Deep Within

By Kris Barringer

How Do You Feel?

Have you ever felt so down that you don't want to exist anymore? Like, did your spirit just change and want you to give up on life? Have you felt so alone that you realize that no one actually cares for you the way God cares/loves me? Would you rather feel nonexistent or become nonexistent? Confused?

My anger is like an ocean, while my pain is like the sea. My lioness is like the lake, while my tiredness flows like the river. My distress aggravation runs like your average creek while my happiness is as small as a pond, yet my love is like a swamp while the joy I have left is like any average pool, yet my faith comes as an average spring season rain. Dare to dig a little deeper in my mind?

As each day goes by, I look forward to eating and getting high afterward, for a day without both is like waking up unappreciative of life. It's the feeling of having no purpose in life, for I have no reason to still wake up every morning since I have nothing to look forward to in life but to get high if not food and the feeling of sex. I have family, some I know, others I met before, and the majority I'll never cross paths with, nor do I know who is who on both sides of my family, and they can walk right past me and not know who you are so I'm left feeling/ being alone. I put myself around other associates to feel something I once felt when my granny was still alive, yet I'm left with a memory both good and bad. That still doesn't change the fact that I walk into an empty house where I have no one to talk to, cry on, or even a simple hug, which I always wanted/longed for both my parents to do, mainly my mom, though. I know there's a God, and I write my thoughts in a notebook praying that God understands/ hears me with my cries, hurt, pain, troubled mind, yet I'm still not satisfied, well, at least my emotional feelings aren't.

Loneliness

In a dark room with a candle glowing in the darkness, yet no one's around to recognize the light. She's all alone, with nowhere to go and no one to seek for. In her eyes, she sees people walking past her while others walk through her, yet no one notices her, not her tears, nor do they feel or see her. No one even hears her cries. Instead, she sees everyone around her laughing, smiling, and talking to others. She sees people holding hands, not having to be/feel alone like her, and how she feels. However, mentally she also sees and hears others like her with tears and scars on their faces with the prettiest, sparkling eyes glowing through it all with the same candle glowing. How long shall she be and feel and see these things around her and do nothing about it? She's weak herself and no longer wants to bear it all. She's afraid that she may lose faith and hope that she was born with, and that the candlelight will soon go out and no one will ever see her or the light if someone comes looking for her.

She has felt this way for some time, and it lingers on her arm and down her chest to her feet. She has slowly embraced the new feelings she now feels or doesn't know how or what to do to escape it all. She longs for joy, peace, happiness that she once felt before, but as the first twenty-three years went by, she learned, saw, witnessed things that led the god-like things to somehow escape from her and have been replaced with the opposite feelings she's supposed to feel. Look into her heart, and you will see broken pieces of a girl hiding behind her smile and laughter when she should substitute it with tears and the cries that came before it.

Trust And Pain

I grew up trusting and believing in everything and everyone I've seen. However, as I got to the age that I am now as I write this book, I've concluded that the only person I trust and can only trust is God Himself. I put others through my personal test, and my trust is at its limits with others depending on who you are as a person and what role/position you play in my life to determine your trust limitation. This world itself showed me both bad and good, yet the bad, of course, troubles me. It's sadder when you do things out of love, and their actions make you have the spirit of feeling regretful. Not only that, but the person who hurt you in any way leaves a hurt as pure and as deep as the love you originally had for the person.

Because of the things I've gone through in the past as far as the hurt and the pain, I must now feel only a pinch of how God felt at the time and all He saw, knew, and went through before my time and after. The key question will be the "Why will someone want to hurt, betray you to simply just being taken advantage of?" The most logical thing I can come up with close to an answer is that they are only truly out for themselves, especially those who put themselves before anything, regardless of the situation. I tend to put others before me, similar to how God has put us before Him by coming to earth just to die in the hands of sinners only for us to be forgiven and believe in him so that we may have a chance of eternal life through His beloved son, Jesus Christ.

If that's not real love, the same love I crave from both my parents as I water this book, the love I want/need from my family on all four sides, the love I want from my siblings, or the love I once felt and gave out to one another whomever I ever crossed paths with. I don't know or understand what love is or feels like. Unfortunately for those who don't receive my love anymore, they clearly did something that offended, hurt, betrayed, or simply proved to me why not to trust them. I refuse to give or show them the love I want to show them, for I fear that my love will continue to be taken for granted. What I mean by that is as people around me show and give me hurt/pain in any type of way, shows me visually (since I'm a visual learner) that they're physically taking pieces of my heart that I gave them, used it mentally or emotionally and throws it on the ground when they're done using it.

Some will step on it while others will spit on it. Some come back for more, yet all parties throw it in the trash and walk off, not even looking back, nor recognize nor feel sorry for what they've done as if I can continue to keep this cycle going until I die. Do they not know my heart is getting weaker and weaker each time? Do they not know that it messes with me mentally and emotionally, leading to the physical stages? I become more afraid and distant, isolating myself from the world back into the same shell I once came out of growing up.

Unfortunately for me, this is the stage I am currently at in my life as I write this book, yet I've been told twice in one week that love conquered all. I'm just now realizing, believing in that statement only because of God and the love He gave to us we didn't, don't, or never will deserve. That's where we ought to humble ourselves. In which right do we have that God had or should do what He's doing for us now? Since we all know the answer to that question, I feel if God Himself can do it and show love to me and others that I at least ought to try to love others, yet it's not nor will never be as close as God's unconditional genuine love. However, God recently inspired me in due time when I'm ready to slowly try.

I've also concluded that I must first pluck the plank in my eye first so that I may clearly see the other plank in my brother/sister's eye. Translation to that is that I need to first fix myself before I want/need to fix the next person, whether they are my enemy. The love I will give, I will give differently. Meanwhile, I'm still at the "isolation" stage of the world, back in the same shell due to not having no one to trust and refusing to fully trust another human being created by God. I put it as the "I trust you as far as I can see you," yet the world itself taught me that even what you see is or can be deceiving. Salt may look like sugar, but you won't know which until you taste it, minus how it looks or feels. It led me to trust no one and nothing, and each time I tried to ignore the message and still believe and trust someone, it backfired every time and laughed in my face telling me, "I told you so." Is this how God feels every time I fail Him? Is it crazy how He still loves/blesses and is merciful to his people and me?

One of the many things about Him and me is that I'm afraid and develop the spirit of fear inside of me. I now guard my heart and put walls up. Now, I simply watch people, what they say, how they say it, and what they do every time I'm with a person regardless of who you are, what you do, and how you do it. My heart that I fail to give and show to others because it shall be on the floor, all alone, with no one to love it or, better yet, love me. The only love I will genuinely show and know will illustrate it back to me and not be afraid to do/show love to be and forever will be kids. Even when they don't fully understand you, they still sense certain things, from someone in pain to someone afraid. Their love is also pure and genuine, and they have lots of love to give and adore one another, something I used to do and feel at their age. Yet again, as I have gotten older, the world showed and taught me things that weren't taught in school, from pre-K to college. It was better showed to me than verbally explained to me thanks to God showing and allowing me to see and experience and feel better than just telling me, for he knows how hard-headed I can get, something I need to change in due time.

God Himself showed me/let me realize that the ones closest to you can/will hurt you just so you may understand how God Himself felt since Satan betrayed him, which started this whole lifetime b.s. I see now why jealousy is one of the seven deadliest sins. Then Jesus was betrayed by Judas even after Jesus himself let Judas know he was about to betray Him. So if it happened to God twice, it shouldn't be that much of a surprise if/when it happens to us all.

In my case, it went from my mom to my ex-best friend that betrayed, hurt, and caused pain and bad memories that are difficult to escape from or forget, let alone to forgive and let go. The pain, however, taught me several lessons, and when I made the same mistakes repeatedly, God showed me that the pattern would have the same results unless you were to do something different about the battered.

What makes it so special is that when I repeated the same mistakes, God was patient enough with me to let Him repeat Himself and the lesson until I understood what He already knew. Shoot, taking it from my mom, I disliked repeating myself simply because I used to get hit when my mom had to repeat herself. Parents and others who have ever hurt you in the past and caused you pain messes with your mind mentally and emotionally. Once you feel hurt or pain of any kind, you then look at life and people and things differently. Not only that, but you act differently and live life differently from how you look at life before the pain first hit you, whether physically or mentally.

The world led me to see and believe in no one or nothing. That you're out here on your own, alone, and if you want things done especially a certain way, you must not be lazy (sloth, which is another deadly sin out of the seven) and do it yourself. That way, you may have a chance to appreciate it more than whatever it is you do/desire to do or have. If you were to fall off track, you need to hop back on as soon as possible, or the world will move forward with or without you, but the world couldn't care less what decision you make, but God can and does.

The sad part is once you're down to your last and you have no help or no support, it's hard to get back up, let alone have someone in your corner to motivate and encourage you. It seems even more challenging once you've gotten comfortable/used to/immune to the tragic change, and once you've gotten too comfortable/ lazy, it's impossible to get back up and start from where you were left. Yet with God, the impossible to Him is saying I'm possible with God and what He can do, for there's nothing He can't do. I'm a strong, brave walking testimony/witness of what God did for me and all my past, impossible from birth to still being alive today.

As I write this book, and to this day, the doctors are confused about how I'm still alive after expecting to die by the age of five. However, nineteen years after my expected death date, I'm still here, and no one understands it nor how, yet what's understood to God doesn't need to be explained to us. It's understood that there's a God, and technically there is no need to explain that He is God, yet he shows us through the many blessings He blesses us all with each day, from waking us up to putting us to sleep. In other words, this galaxy, earth, water, animals, and humans do not or never will operate on their own whether God is an energy, force, and spirit act (however you wish to put it). Clearly, He's running the show. We all have front seats to watch and learn.

Talking about God Himself makes my spirit feel better on the inside by having and keeping the faith that I still have that I finally have someone and something to look forward to after all this life has to offer is over and done with. In the meantime, I'm stuck in this lifetime dealing with people plus my health/ emotion, and that's enough on my plate. I've recently learned that no matter what, we will have to go through trials and tribulations, but to remain of good cheer for Jesus (God) overcame the world, and what we went/go through can't compare to what God will bless us all with. However, being honest, it's easier said than done. Being raised in Cleveland, Ohio, let alone the fifty states of America, I know I'm far from the only person who sees life the way I've looked at life after being exposed to all sorts of pain.

It all started from pain rather than death to betrayal as I look back on life. In some cases, betrayal can hurt more than death itself. Being betrayed is simply said that the person you once trusted and loved showed you how you're the fool to have even trusted the person who betrayed/ hurt you. It shows you that no one thinks or moves the way you think and will move. Since you now realize that there's only one of you who thinks and moves the way you think and move, who you can trust and only trust, you again notice that life is now different from what you first assumed.

That's our fault for assuming, for if you spell assume, it spelled ASS U-N-ME, meaning you're making an ass out of you and me for assuming. You feel like the world is against you and that everyone is out for themselves when there are still good people here, yet some of them will change (me) due to life and its many wicked ways. The other half remains the same, yet the mind is not, and once that happens, you have a battle with both your heart and your mind being on the same team.

In my case, my heart wants to love and help make a person smile, helping them in any type of way I can, yet since I've been exposed to "life", my mind tells me not to remain the same person as I was before unless I desire to commit suicide to a spirit who just wanted to love and be loved. I know and am very convinced that God Himself loves me unconditionally but do my parents love me for me, or do they love what I can do/did for my parents? Do my friends love me the way I once loved them? However, I can honestly say that I know a friend I've known since a teenager that has love for me, and she shows it well. She asks for nothing but my time and company. Neither has she shown signs for me not to befriend her, unlike the other people I've crossed paths with both before and after her. I've literally sat and watched her just as the other ex-friends I've had and compared them on how they treated me versus how I've treated them. Of course, I've realized that being in this world, especially when you experience the world alone as if it's you versus the world versus God, you find out that everyone around you isn't there for you but for themselves.

Besides God Himself, every one of my past friends showed me they did not love me. They'd rather love to use me for their own good, except for that one female friend. People call her Fanny, and I thank God for her because she's someone I want to be spirit-wise, and even though I'm older than her, I look up to her in a way. With the heart she has, I desperately want back that of which I can only receive from God. Not to get off subject, going back to the no love I receive, I also feel that no love b.s. from my six siblings, yet I blame both my parents for the lack of love they show toward one another, including me.

The three siblings I grew up with were as close as white on rice, yet as the years went by, so did the distance. It found its way, and now our relationship/ love toward one another is now miles and miles away. I have an older brother I once looked up to and did everything with, from fights to experimenting with different ways of sex to dealing with my mom and her many issues. Yet again, as the years went by, I could no longer look at him the same.

Don't get me wrong. I love my older brother to death and back. I recently forgave him this year, from 2015, for all the b.s. and drama he put me through and dealt with. He used me and left me when I needed him the most, knowing that I had no other help from no one else. Especially when he up and left me in the house by myself after my second surgery on my left shoulder, which I had forty-eight hours prior after my little sister on my dad's side went home, leaving me to fine for myself. To make it no better, no one on all four sides of the family offered a helping hand nor wanted to help (out of love), leaving me to go back to a nursing home as if I was cool being there.

Going through that process mentally alone took the little love I had left and replaced it with pain, disappointment, loneliness, helplessness, forgotten, and an unloved feeling. As far as my mom's two youngest kids (since their minors as I write this book) and is under my mom's harsh/angry/mean ways, my little sister is currently going through what I've gone through when it comes to dealing with my mom growing up yet, she's off the hook. Still, again I blame our mom for spoiling both my younger siblings while my brother and I were their slaves/servants while our mom and our two siblings were the three slave masters.

The point I'm trying to make now is that our mom is messing us up mentally with the emotions and actions, one by one. Not forgiving and letting go of the pain and hurt she's caused in the past allows her to continue to control my life and emotions and has been for some time. I act like her in more ways than expected, yet I can't stay in a room with her without wanting to run away or think of the hurt and pain in the past, and boom, before you know it, I've cried me a river into a sea leading to the ocean. I've consumed so much that I don't know how to let it out without fighting someone to vandalize something. Still, the scars from my mind and body to soul remain after all is said and done. Since there's no love in the home, all hope of a happy family (I once had), peace, joy, love all went out the door.

My family may have a love for me (only God knows the real me), but they never show it nor say it, minus the few people on my dad's side of the family. So if I didn't receive the love and care at home or from friends, how can I love myself and others? Now I do love and recently accepted myself for who I am as a person, but due to the lack of love given to me, it is the reason I act the way I act today.

As I write this book, I have everyone around me for how I act and feel, and my mom plays a significant role in it. The lack of love I had in my heart has been misplaced somewhere. Instead, it has been replaced with pain, hurt, betrayal, being stepped on, laughed at, disappointment, disrespected, no expectations, lioness, hatred, revengeful, harden heart, tired, fed up, frustrated, hopeless, lifeless, doubtful, all equaling to me feeling that my life is pointless here on earth. Yet, who am I to tell God that my life is meaningless, even though I felt the way I currently feel as I was becoming an adult? My happy moments and memories in the past will soon disappear and be replaced with all the sad, hurtful, painful, confusing memories I've recently felt and experienced, and I dwell on it all. Since I live a solitary life going to an empty house daily that I refuse to call home, I have all day and night to think and allow my mind to run wild — something the world should have never allowed me to do. I've thought so much that I'm writing it all in a book to see if at least one person can feel and understand me besides God Himself.

First thing first being alone is a feeling no one wants/needs to feel, and unfortunately for me, I'm in a world/city full of people I see and speak to daily, from my neighbors to strangers to social media to my fam (the ones I do talk to once in a blue moon). Yet, I still feel alone and that no one cares that I feel the way I feel as I write this book. I know God is with me at all times, yet since I can't see him just yet or feel his hugs I desperately want/need, I feel alone, and all I'm stuck with is prayer while God constantly shows me how much He loves me through the blessings while my generation does the opposite.

We don't use the actual definition of love the way God uses the word love, especially relationship-wise. Instead of showing each other that they love one another like God does and show us, we tend to tell one another that we love one another. So here I am, walking the earth, partying with different people, just to return to an empty house just for reality to hit you and tell/show how alone you really are and have been.

At first, I was used to the family I was born to on my mom's side of the family. I even had the fantasy dream house, which includes my number one grandparents, with their five kids and their kids, and that's where I come in. We all live in a mansion with our nine dogs, my great grandparents, and their other two daughters with their kids and grandkids. I bet, more like guarantee if we lived life the way God wanted/ intended us to live how much fun and love we'll have for one another, yet that's why this is still my fantasy. Yet as reality kicks in, the family I want and what my heart desires don't exist, so the love I needed from them isn't here. Instead of looking/searching for it through a family member to a friend, I damn near find it from a male companion and want it from a baby of my own, possibly four, whom I can show my love to so they may cherish it and share their love with me.

Mentally, though, I'll just be using them to replace the love I lust to receive from my family members I feel I no longer have. I would replace the family absence with new love from my kids since I can no longer feel it from the people who have hurt me in the past to betray something God felt from His own ex-best friend. The funny thing about this is that I never cared for companionship growing up and never seemed it since I witnessed my mom getting cheated on, me witnessing males in my family cheat on their significant others from my uncle to my brother. Thanks to my big brother, I wasn't allowed, nor could I have a boyfriend until he left me when I was fifteen, which was the beginning of our new relationship change.

Even after my brother left, the boyfriends I had on the low, I never took them seriously, and they showed me in due time reasons not to reconsider a relationship with a guy serious. I was hipped fast to the misleading games people tend to play. By the time I was legal by law, not only was I hipped, but by the age of eighteen, I'd witness everyone around, from boys to classmates to everyone I've crossed paths with, no matter how I met you. Ninety-nine percent have shown me not to trust or believe in them and say screw them. I did just that, and to this day, it's the same agenda mentality, and it dwells through me, in me, and all around me.

How a person treats you lets, you know how the person is. All I ever wanted was to be a kid and to remain a kid, as I first remembered being alive for the first time. The difference between back then and now is that my list gets shorter and shorter, and I'm now stuck with a choice/ decision to love a baby of my own just to love them the way I needed/ wanted to be loved by my mom. I'm very convinced that my parents love me only because there's a God, yet I'm not convinced enough that they love me for me.

Over the next five years after being considered as an adult, I've been walking a loveless, heartless life living in this world searching for missing pieces that will/shall fix what's been broken already in me, not realizing or thinking about God nor what is meant for me to still be here/alive and not dead like I was supposed to twenty-three years ago. Although I'm not sure why I'm still here, I have a clue and if it's for me to speak, write, motivate people, and brag about God, then let it be in his WILL for me to complete. I need this light way to feel alive on the inside and become more happy, grateful to wake up every morning. Plus, I've been told several times by several people that I'm an excellent self-motivator, and I love how I can help a person, from talking to them to advising them to being the shoulder they need to cry on. God bless me with a heart to want to help and love others, so blame/award Him for what I'm trying to do to my readers.

Before I can say anything, you first need to understand me to feel where I'm coming from. I told you a little about me, yet I have to dig a little deeper so you all can really feel me and not just hear me. First, you must understand where I've come from, what I've been through, how I look at life now, and how my past affected my present and future. Those who have read my two books, *Behind Every Smile* and *Walking Testimony*, should hopefully have a clear picture of where I came from and what I've been through. However, I'm not convinced that my readers feel nor look at life how I look at life, but how the world made me look at life. Not going too far back in my life, I will let you guys know and understand how my mind works before I tell you what I really want/need to tell you about life, especially for those who do not live how we "street people" live life, so you'll never imagine how the world is revealed in our eyes.

Again, before I say more, let me take you inside my mind so you can know and understand what God and myself know and understand. I will not go too deep nor open up to the world on my thoughts or how my mind can get, yet you shall exasperate how to be deep with my mind and get you to focus on your mind and what's really deep within it.

Feelings Growing Up

I grew up not loving my mom because she stopped showing me love. Instead, she showed she didn't love me but loved using me to please/satisfy her, from cleaning, massages, and bringing in money as if I were an object with no feelings nor care to be loved. Since she showed me I was only here as her servant and not her first daughter, I looked for love elsewhere. However, it taught me that no love existed through the many associates I used to love over the years. The majority used me, several were fake, some fell off over petty things, others became distant, and a lot just disrespected me in my three reasons I fight category, so you know how that goes, and the rest showed me how I couldn't trust them.

I know a person who has a heart like mine and reminds me of myself. Our stories are relatable, from how her mom treated her to having the same emotions inside, to how she doesn't mess with her family to her helping others, and I adore her so much. However, she, too, has her fake ways, despite realizing her heart is similar to mine. Still, the world taught me to trust no one and constantly expect the unexpected. What do I mean by all this? Let me explain by digging deeper inside my mind.

Growing up, I was mentally okay. I was born a happy child and was told about God. I went to my family church, going out to the hometown buffet or Mr. Chicken with my granny afterward. We would then travel the world in the summer, from Florida to California to Canada with my great-grandpa and his family. And because he was married to my great grandma, who I never met before, her siblings and their families up to for generations would travel to these places with us, and yes, we travel deep. So again, mentally, I was thrilled with what life had to offer. There was nothing but love and happiness with laughter and fun memories, especially with the holidays and parties I was allowed to attend as a kid.

I kept in mind, though, that there was a guy who used to visit my granny's house, and one day, he suddenly stopped. I never asked what happened to him, nor did anyone explain what happened to him. I also remember seeing a picture of his face in my mom's room but never dared to ask why this picture there or what happened to him was coming back over my granny's house, so I left the curious convocation alone. I knew my dad, what he looked like, and knew I had two other siblings from him and his new family. Still, I barely saw him, and I was ok with that, especially with my mom getting married, and my granny recorded it.

Mentally in my head, I recognized, or realized, as I should say, that a man can love a woman and have a bae. I only thought that was for my grandparents and great grandpa, although his wife was dead before I arrived here on earth. Again, that was what made me happy at the time, and I never wanted for anything since everything I needed was right in front of me, and I was satisfied. It seemed like I had a reason to wake up every morning because I looked forward to seeing my family and the smile on their faces back then.

As a toddler, I seemed like a good kid. Yet, as I grew older, I knew I was a bad child yet never cared or paid attention to how my mom felt as well as God Himself since He had begotten all of us as His kids and only have been a begotten father to His beloved son Jesus. Still, the life I was living at the time, I assumed, was the life that I was meant to live by and for. I believed my purpose was just to be a kid to my family and never grow old, nor will the fun of being a kid will never end nor drift away. Imagine one of your happy moments lasting a year each. Sometimes I couldn't believe nor accept that I was even alive, for I never knew or realized I could exist.

The things I've seen and remembered weren't believable at the time because it was too good to be considered authentic. So again, mentally, my mind knew no such thing as hurt, pain, betrayal, loneliness, helplessness at the time. Still, as I went from five to eight, I felt my first real pain besides the countless whippings I got from my mama to my great papa and everyone in between. However, the day my granny died, my life changed, and it has never been the same, not even close to it.

Mentally, my mind received its first scar. Before my granny's death, I've been in countless fights to going to the psychiatric hospital at Cleveland Clinic on the sixth floor. Still, none of that fazed me nor my hand at the time, and I sometimes ignored my disability, plus when my granny always told me I wasn't disabled, something my mom should have been doing. However, on February seventh of the year 2000, things took a turn for the worse, and that day, I knew there was a thing such as death, pain, and hurt. I didn't know how to deal with it mentally, yet I still believed in God. I was first hurt, then angry at the world as the years went by without her. Instead, I held in my true emotions and maintained school and the kids. Those who read my past book (*Behind Every Smile)* know how my school life went. I fought, dealt with people, and explained how my mom treated me differently and stopped loving me the way she used to love me before my granny died. So mentally, my mom, my happy life, and my family died with my granny.

Over the following months, the distance took its role, and we all slowly grew up separately. My granny left her husband, sisters, father, kids, and grandkids and took our lover and hearts with her and buried it all. Consequently, it was the beginning stages of searching for love in the wrong places with the wrong people. I first assumed they all were my friends and loved ones. Again, people only showed and told me they only care for themselves. Still, the majority have families and relationships with their mothers, freedom, and not getting treated how my mom was treating me. The things my mom did in the past made pathetic pain, and all the tears I've cried created more pain and hurt that turned into anger I emotionally developed after my granny died. The people outside my family didn't make my life any better, and I became angrier more mentally isolated, and I held it all in until graduation.

I never showed others how I really felt growing up unless I broke down in school in the twelfth grade or the countless fights that I've been in from fighting a guy or girl with my one hand. Most fights were with my brother and me as we were going to the same schools growing up before we were separated. So mentally, I was observing everything like a sponge and figuring out how to deal with what problems as I slowly digested it inside my flesh. Now, I will remember the things people did to me, both good and bad. It is hard for me to forget it even if I wanted to.

I can remember every year that has passed me up to 2015 as I write this book. For some odd reason, I have a strange memory that will remember a specific date and time of an event no matter how far along it was. However, I'll use my memory to take precautions to avoid the same hurt, mistakes, pain twice, and unfortunately, I've failed. I've been exposed to disappointment, betrayal, being used, taken advantage of, taking for granted, disrespected, useless, loveless, that no one cares, fuck the world, loneliness, heartache. Plus, the pain I've been feeling over the last fifteen years is causing my mind to be on the verge of self-destructing because it refuses to deal with the persistent pattern of ungod-like things, whether or not it had a choice to.

Mentally, I was feeling fucked up, and evilness crept in. I was slowly feeling the wicked ways and stepping into the dark side of what God wanted me to turn from, for my wicked thoughts have nothing on God's wrath (if He decides or when He shows his true definition of anger, I believe he will soon come). Since He made me and I have my own wicked/evil ways and thoughts with revenge, I'm quite sure God Himself knows the definition of revenge and knows it well. It makes sense that God wants us to flee from our wicked ways, and just like God plays for keeps, so do I, although my revenge definition may differ from

God's definition of revenge, even though we still will play for keeps.

At the time of first becoming a young adult, I was going off my mind more than my heart at the wrong time and situations where I should have used my mind every time I was to use my heart and vice versa. I never looked at things or situations I've been through as lessons at first, then once I got the picture of the lesson and the moral of the lesson, evil ways and wicked thoughts came along. I came revengeful, getting back at all who hurt me and showing people the actual definition of being a heartless person. Since I felt no one cared for or about me, but a few, whom I thought cared at the time, I felt they wanted me to treat them how they treat me and others, and if ruthless was what the world wanted, so shall it be, and I didn't care how ruthless I acted and can get.

Again, no one understands me but a few of what I was going through as far as me being a child growing up in my mom's house for if they understood me and how I felt, how different people would have treated me from school to my workplaces to the strangers in the street to my own family. They would have helped fix me mentally, having me conclude that there are still some good people in the world. Instead, I have seen the world for what it really is and how real it can get thanks to the help of others trying and attempting to destroy me, for I may bend a little, but I won't fold. Imagine everything you first saw and felt growing up being taken from you one by one and replaced with new things that are the opposite of what you were used to, and it lasts longer than the good. It's just like writing a pro/con list on your spouse, yet they can outweigh the pros.

Meanwhile, you're going to do just about anything to get rid of the cons when you've had enough of the hurt and pain and are now tired of feeling the way you feel, knowing it isn't pleasing or pleasant. Once you realize you no longer want to feel the way you currently feel, you make a change just to change the outcome. You hope deep inside that it brings back all the god-like things you first felt before the pain and wish for the same old emotions you used to feel with another person/opportunity. Yet, I failed in that category as well.

By the age of eighteen, I had the mindset of saying fuck people, don't trust them, you can't love anyone, not even your own family on all four sides love you the way you would want to love them, for their love to you is not the same love God shows to us all. Your way away from life and its drama was through school and school only. By eighteen, my mind was set on attending Akron University, staying on campus for the next four years, and by then, God will be finally leading me to where I was made to be led to.

Still, four years after my graduation, I went down a path I should have seen coming miles away, and for those who read my second book (*Walking Testimony),* you as well as I know exactly what I'm referring to as far as where I went from and where I was trying to head at my life. When you add failure, disappointment, setbacks, and reroutes to the mentally that's already been disturbed and distressed, the emotional list becomes longer and longer as the years get old. It goes from me just being in disbelief to hopeless yet being me in a world full of people who I act or look like how I feel on the inside. For I prefer people not to know me for the spirit of fear to be on me as far as others taking me and my life hurts and pain as a weakness, which is clearly an underestimated gesture the others have made. And again, for those who read my two books, you'll witness how many times someone underestimated me because of my disability, so imagine me acting and looking the way I actually feel on the inside, or how many times I will have to prove a point. Not only does no one know how I feel or understand me, but I honestly believe no one would even care about me and my feelings simply because everyone cares about their own wants/needs and likes/dislikes. In doing so, they fail to have time to think about others, not even at least considering another's thoughts or feelings.

In this generation, the way we live and are as individuals alone tells one another that we tend to care for ourselves more than we care for another person other than them. Yet, God never intended us to become such people as we are today, including me, for I'm not a perfect person until I'm right with God. I have my share of skeletons in my closet that only God and I will know about, for there's not one perfect person walking among the earth in this lifetime, not to mention this generation. Unfortunately for some, they're not even trying to change their chapter, for they don't care to change. The same way that my mind is now set up to where it's at a stage where it no longer cares about nothing nor no one on top of being fed up, tired, hurt, betrayal act. The moral of the story is that my mind has consumed so much that its path is crooked, and it has to protect the heart so that I can survive as a human living in this lifetime surrounded by my generation.

From eighteen to twenty-three, I went from having something to having nothing twice by being in the situation with my brother and a person I used to call my buff. My mom let me fend for myself after sending me to jail countless times for different reasons, including the countless times she called the police just to get me out of the house after paying rent.

I had my first house in the twelfth grade, which was dumb rule number one. I experienced more death, fewer friends, feeling like a stranger in a place I shall call home, and figuring out how I'll live my life and the purpose of me still being alive. I've been exposed to drugs, and if I wanted to, I could easily start selling dope like my other street friends just to make income to solve money problems. I call myself having money problems because I receive SSI checks and food stamps, and I'm supposed to make a living happily ever after. What was I supposed to do with my life with a $700 SSI check and barely $200 food stamp card? What's the purpose of me living if I'm just supposed to receive an SSI check and food assistance and live happily ever after as if that's a comfortable way to live being on limitations and restrictions? The receiving handout part is good, but it isn't enough to satisfy me or my heart. Then I still have love for my family, and their love for me is not the same love I give to them, while others around me take my love for granted. So, let me first ask you, how would you feel being in my shoes walking the same path I've walked and felt the same way I feel?

Even though I was now looking at life differently and felt different with all the evil emotions under it all, you will see it's clearly all from pain. Yet underneath the pain is still a small piece of my heart that was left looking, searching for love from something, someone anyone to love me not realizing I should give my love to God and have faith he'll turn that those broken pieces and trade it in for better/renewed heart. My mind, however, I would have wished for a different one, yet for some reason, it fits me perfectly and how I live my life as of today. I could also be using the right tools for the wrong reasons, especially living in the hood.

To maintain it all in my head and still manage to smile and act goofy around others was just an act of how I really wanted to feel on the inside. I desperately wanted help, yet I wasn't as comfortable as I should have been with letting others know how I really felt. It could have been taken as pain. I didn't realize the pain, hurt, and distress turned into anger, which made me the tough little girl I am today. That famous saying, "my pain is my preparation for my destination", which I am unaware of at this point as I write this book.

All the betrayal, disloyal, disrespectful ways, and hatred toward me all bottled inside me, and the only I could or would let it out was through the many opportunities I had to fight another person. Even though it was technically an unfair fight, since I only used one hand to fight in my eyes, my one hand did just as much damage as a person could do with two hands. I can proudly/boldly say I never got my behind beat up, even though I fight with my one hand and do not plan to meet anyone who will, so my fighting days may be over. Let just God will show you better than he shall tell you to stop the fighting, and let's just say I would never forget the feeling of a dislocation, let alone the mental stage of not having the use of either arm.

Besides, I know only God and Jesus are the biggest, boldest that ever existed.

However, even after a fight, anyone can heal physically, but the damage to one's mind can't be held. It's a scar maybe but never healed, especially in my case where you have no choice but to remember the pain and try to handle it all, yet you're immune to it now, walking on eggshells trying not to break even more. Sometimes it's hard, for I had my shares of breakthroughs and breakdowns, yet thanks to the grace of God, I still manage to live twenty-three years of life and not fold even after the doctor told my mom I wasn't supposed to see the age of five followed by the struggle. I've struggled my entire life, yet if you were to meet me in person, you would never think or consider I had a hard life or what I've been through. Again, I don't act how I feel. Outside my heart are depression, feelings of failure and disappointment, and pain from being hurt physically and emotionally, from my mom and the beatings to her mentally hurtful words from my granny's death.

Over the years, the emotions were guarded by fire to block the same emotions, plus others were getting closer to my heart. However, the fire was also there to keep emotions inside me as a reminder of what to expect from others and to ember how it felt to feel the way you did as far as all the ungod-like things and feelings. That explains the first tattoo on my right arm. I have a heart to love and be loved, help, and give to others, yet how the world is set up and the things I've witnessed tell me I'm going to regret it every time I was to go by my heart and not by my mind. So what does the heart tell the mind? Not to trust nor expect honesty, respect, trust, believe, help, cherish, depend on, love, help no one or I will regret it, and my heart will tell my mind, "I told you so you, fool".

With my heart and mind now informed on what to do and what not to do, what to expect and not expect, it hides itself away. It departs from everything and everyone.

Once the mind realizes the change, it's notified by the heart that both the mind and the heart are alone, deep within the body, departed to be saved, yet don't want to be found. (Confused?) Both the mind and the heart play the role of a human being alone, unloved, un-cared for, unimportant, useless, and hopeless. It becomes selfish, harsh, isolated, wicked thoughts and ways yet desperate to change, but afraid it will only worsen than what it already is if I can allow myself to be found and rescued.

This Cinderella turned into her evil stepmom or Maleficent in Sleeping Beauty. Although you may believe Maleficent was evil for doing what she did to Sleeping Beauty yet, did anyone care about how she became the evil witch to why or what made her turn evil in the first place? Just as her, so it is to me, for I turned from the happy little joyful girl I was born to be into all the people who hurt me in the past, from my mom, brother, and fake friends to the niggas I have sex with. No one is born evil, yet the actions of others around that person can dangerously control the person and their actions that others have affected. Their actions are done to the person they just harmed, not realizing that the pain and hurt they just now received can turn into anger or wrath in five seconds, especially when there's no justice being served. Your revengeful ways just want to seek the justice it feels it deserves.

Can you now say it's your fault for how you now feel? No, blame those around you who helped cause you pain, just like I blame those around me for my actions. Still, I can't let their actions determine my actions, yet it affects my feelings, emotions, and sometimes enough is enough, and you begin to feel fed up to the max. You'll never know what you will or won't do until you're actually in that situation. Decision-making in its rawest form can determine where your mind is at and what your heart is set on. Since the world or its people taught/raised me to trust no one nor love them, how should my mind interpret that? To only care about me and to worry about myself, no one will help you in your time of need but you. Looks are deceiving. It's you by yourself against the world, for it's you yourself versus the world, have no hope, faith in others, expect the unexpected, do unto others as they do to you, or it's a sign of weakness, and people will walk over you if you sit around and do nothing about it. No one loves or cares about you, not even your parents to the niggas you sleep with, meaning fall back and go ghost on people.

That mentally slowly took its role in my mind due to all I was going through, but more into protecting myself since now, I felt unsafe in an untrusted world. Experiencing what I experienced and those who read my two stories know what I'm talking about. It changes the way you used to think, and now you wonder what you first were taught was actually true, or was it all a lie from birth? Then my disability and fear of my tumor returning, or my disability worsening makes me worry if I'll completely lose my ability to move my right side of the body as I get older? Is my disability going to be the downfall in my life? Then I concluded that if and when I need help, no one is nor will ever be there for me, so why should I be around people? Is it the way they make me feel? I drink and smoke alone and others for the feeling and memories of it all. The feeling of being intoxicated, dancing to the music, being around others, whether or not you mess with them, making everything in life at that time seem better, will at least you can make the best of the situation. It makes/allows you to escape reality, and besides sleep, it's an easy way to escape the hurt, pain, anger I feel inside.

I keep myself high, especially alone for the feeling of it alone. It makes any situation you're in feel/seem better since it's a way to escape the hurt and pain. Instead of cutting myself, I use sex, weed, liquor, and partying to feel better inside and keep the memory of what I enjoyed at the moment. I need my readers to understand the way I think by feeling/understanding the way I feel first before I can express my opinion on how I look at life based on other facts this world in their people put it as, as well as the different situations and circumstances. Understand why I trust no one. Understand why I feel/am alone. Understand why I don't feel loved. Understand why I can't love/ trust anyone. Understand the pain I carry on the inside.

Understand why I have trust issues. Feel how I feel/felt. Understand why I am the person I am today.

Instead of being the usual outside of the window looking in, let's trade places. You become the inside of the window looking out the window while I notice from the outside looking in as I'm trying to look at others how they looked at me from the old me and my mouth to how I react to certain situations. I'm convinced that others look at my life as corny/non-complicated because of a check, and technically, all I have to do is spend it on living a life I can afford. They feel receiving handouts is the life to live, and I strongly disagree. It could be the life for others who don't want to strive and aim for greatness, but not for me. I love that the previous statement is true and that I can become lazy in life and sit on my behind and wait until I die, but my soul wants more than the flesh it has been assigned to. Not only do I believe in God, but I believe He kept me here this long for His own reason, but also for my sake.

I want/need to have a purpose for living. I want a daily goal/agenda or exigent. I need a reason to wake up every morning since pleasing my family hasn't worked out. Without this drive or ambition of having a purpose of waking up every morning, weakness in my heart/spirit messes with my mind daily, and depression creeps its way into my mind. Of course, being on the outside looking in, you can't or won't see it how I see it unless I was to express my feelings about it.

The fact that I can't do my own hair pisses me off. Now honestly, I can do simple stuff from washing my hair to flat ironing my hair, but the simple fact that I can't do more from braiding to a ponytail makes me feel less of a person, and that's when my disability really kicks in. The fact that I was never taught to ride a bike, nor can I teach someone to do it, pisses me off to the soul, all thanks to my mind sending hateful messages to my heart saying, *"you can't do it,"* slowly teasing my heart on what the flesh can and can't do. Because of my limitation on my right hand and foot, it will feel like I'm less helpful than expected. Yet,

I can say I can tie my shoes thanks to my granny to knowing how to fight and defend myself when needed to roll my own blunts, yet the feeling of not accomplishing everything I should have accomplished (if I was normal) messes with me, yet I let no one know.

I've always had to constantly show the tough side to other people to let them know I was far from weak and not to be messed with. Often, I felt the need to prove myself to others, from fighting to cracking jokes just so they could understand that I'm just like them with a sense of humor given to me by God. This is why I thank God for all I've gone through with my mom due to the beatings to the starvation. The things she put me through made me tough and geared me up to show it to others since I couldn't express my anger to my mom besides the usual stealing, slashing her tires, to cursing under my breath about my mom, and how I wanted her to suffer and die. I wished and hoped for that on my mom so badly that I even switched her meds. So since I couldn't fight against my mom, I waited for the opportunity to fight others as I was informed that I was now their target, but in my eyes, they were the prey, and I was the predator. Do you think my competitive spirit would not take the challenge knowing what my appointed opponent had to offer? I wish my mom did offer. As if a kid less than my weight can do more damage than my mom, who weighed twice as me at the time... not.

I had enough pain and anger to blow Cleveland, Ohio, up seven times and more. If I have that much anger in me, imagine God's wrath toward his people. It's like a nine-to-five job plus overtime at a job and not getting paid enough to do or manage in this world full of people who showed me that you first have to love yourself and forget about everyone else. Parents love their children to an extent while others love them to death and back, yet when it comes to other than their kids, they couldn't care less about you when the opportunity reveals itself.

After all things good and bad were revealed to me, it hardened my heart as the years have gotten older, and it wants to protect itself, and the mind won't take charge because it wants to think more logically than how it feels. The fact that others think I'm not hipped to their bus tickles my mind, and I now look at everything as a game, and since I'm combative to the game of life, we started since we're all actors, may the best actress break their legs, and it shall be me. I know I desire to want to help and change the world. My mind is now in a survival-for-the-world-type manner, and my spirit wants to follow it instead of the heart. What shall I do then? How should I feel? I feel the only people I'm going to deal with, along with their b.s. is my mom and her other three kids and my own kids, whom God will bless me with one day. As far as others, I no longer care for them but to make it to the next lifetime with Jesus.

There's no more energy in me to care for others, whether they're alive or dead, with a home or homeless. I just don't care anymore, nor will I try to remember the people I crossed paths with, whether a sex buddy or an ex-friend. Although I talk to several associates, I only have love for one person named Fanny, and as far as the rest, I talk to keep myself from boredom and catch up on the latest rumor and drama going through the grapevine.

Since I don't talk to my family nor have a family of my own, I pop up on others from time to time to see what they're doing and their lives just to burn time and watch life pass me by. Most days, I stay by myself and to myself, not speaking to no one. My phone is so dry I forget I have one. Everyone in my past that I crossed paths with, but one showed me their true colors as I sat back and observed each one that I ever crossed paths with. If something were done to me, I wouldn't have done to them. Then it tells me not to be as genuine to them as I would like to be. The majority just lied about random stuff to hear themselves talk. If they were being fake toward another person, they were being fake to me behind my back. Everybody is using everybody, so do you think I'm not about to play the same game? The difference between me and the world is that I act like I don't know what's up as far as relationship-wise, and I'll act like I fuck with you, but this girl fucks with no one. She has a friend she adores because she reminds her of herself and how she used to be before the pain. However, honestly, she distances herself from her friend, fearing that she too will regret befriending her in due time.

I'm praying, but as far as everyone else, Kristalen knows you don't fuck with her how Kristalen would fuck with you, so just as fake as they are toward me, I can sell them the same dream I thought I was going to purchase. Instead of stating the obvious, I pretend and play the role others let me know what to play, how to play it, and how they play their roles to me. It's like getting told a joke, and it's funny the first time, but if you continue to hear the joke, it's not as funny as it was the first time. Or like a woman crying over a guy. She's only going to do it for so long until the tears dry out. Then once there are no more tears, there is no more crying over the same guy, and she knows whether to let the guy continue to make her cry or let him and the hurt and pain go. In my case, I'm simply tired of being tired. I'm tired of the same results, so to keep myself from doing or becoming insane, I take different actions to see or seek different results. Since I'm very petty, thanks to my parents, I'll give you a taste of your own medicine and laugh in your face as you swallow the stuff you assumed I would continue to swallow. It's funnier when it's unexpected. Some people think what's done in the dark won't come into the light. Again, it's like I'm working that nine-to-five job plus the overtime, especially since I have nothing else to do at the time.

I love it when the guys come around and play their parts just so they can fuck me as if I didn't already know what they want from me. It's not like I didn't want the same thing from them. Honestly, I used them for personal reasons, including the dick. I'll even have them thinking they're winning. It's funny knowing things someone fails to know/understand. Like I wonder how God is looking at us, all-knowing our hearts, ambitions, thoughts, and ways and why we do them, especially when you think you can hide the truth. It's always fun to play a game you are familiar with and even funnier when you're good at it. I also realize that people don't like to hear the truth, nor can they tell the truth for their own sake. Well, as far as me, this individual loves to tell it how it is, and she knows she has no one on her side or for her. Until she dies, she simply doesn't care about it anymore or anyone other than her three siblings on her mom's side. And she will always love her mom to earth, regardless of what her mom did. And with who she is as a person, she'll always love her the most, has love for my family, and couldn't care less about anyone else, how they feel, their opinions, thoughts, and concerns about the life people are living right now.

Don't get me wrong, my heart goes out and feels for others who are like me and going through a rough patch, but I couldn't care less about anyone and how they live their lives. What you give out to the world, you shall receive back hopefully, tenfold. I know I'm not the toughest, sexiest, smartest person in the world, but who is besides God Himself? This girl wants to deal with nothing from no one since I have had it up to the sky and back with my mom. I just don't care anymore. The only thing on my mind is waiting to meet God and chilling with Jesus along with my grandparents and the same family I grew up with as a kid before my granny died.

I realize I will never be satisfied in this lifetime for as long as I shall live in this world in this lifetime, nor will I get what my heart desires without help. God is patiently waiting on the next lifetime so she can have the same mindset she once had as a kid growing up before her granny died. All I really want is peace, joy, happiness, and the greatest gift of all, which is love. Since she's stuck being here on earth, left with the remaining people, she won't get what she longs for, so she no longer cares nor seeks it from others. Instead, she simply no longer expects it from others, nor will ever again. My mind is set for disappointment, disloyalty, letting people walk out of my life, and I now simply just sit back and watch others around me and open my mouth when needed.

Honestly, sometimes it's hard to keep my mouth closed, yet I'm currently working on that. I'm so used to failure, pain, and only being out for myself that I've become numb to it and understand why I feel the way I feel now as I write this book. Focusing on what God said he went through helps me realize I'm not the only one who went down paths similar to mine. I know others can relate, and I'm far from the only one. Everyone has their own individual paths that can only fit them. So my question to me is, I wonder why my path is made the way it is now? However, I shall see, and my question will be answered, and I will fully understand everything.

I wonder how my life would be if I had never had my disability? What if my mom wasn't as mean, strict, and crazy as she is now? How would I then be as a child growing in this world and life to an adult? However, that would have played out, and it wouldn't fit into the person I needed to become, especially to fit for this lifetime. Why I'm even alive, let alone exist? What if I came at a different time? How would my mind be set up? My mind then wanders off even deeper, more curious with ideas. When you're living alone, all you can do is think or talk to yourself and question the knowledge you know and want to seek. Your mind is technically something only God knows what it's intended for. We may have ideas, clues, and hints, but only God knows it.

It's already amazing how we use our minds now and more amazing how we could use our minds in many ways, whether known or unknown. You would expect (my readers) that after doing surgery on my head and removing pieces of my left side of the brain, how mentally restated I should be just like the doctors expected me to be. Yet, I'm very intelligent for my age and have a good memory thanks to me being able to put stuff together in remembrance, especially for the things I dream to forget. I can remember dates and times depending on what happened and how it played out, whether good or bad.

I was told by doctors removed a part of my brain where the tumor was, which explained the sudden disability on my right side. Yet mentally, I assumed to be perfectly fine minus the anger, tiredness, frustration, and use the pain, hurt, and the loneliness I've always felt and channel it all out, sucking it up like a sponge and really showing how I felt on the inside in every opportunity I had to fight growing up. The tumor might have messed me up physically and left a permanent scar. Still, the way my life has been set up messed me up mentally, so I feel the spirit is traveling in a messed-up body both physically and mentally, in my opinion. Is my mind supposed to be the way it is right now? Do I really need psychological help from a specialist? Do I need to escape my life, agendas, goals, wants, and needs just to trick myself into believing that is okay when in reality it's far from ok and fine? The world is messed up itself, and we, the people, are messing it up more, but let me not go into details yet about this particular subject I'll speak on later in this book. I just need my readers to get inside my head and feel and understand my mind before I state my opinion on life as I see it.

I really believe that I'm a sensitive/emotional person since I'm always in my feelings. That explains the locket surrounded by fire (that's on my arm). I'm in a dark room seeking to be rescued, but I haven't seen the light or a hero, so I'm currently feeling the opposite of how I should feel. I don't know whether I should now go off emotions and feelings that I feel now or unlock and unleash the other true desirable feelings locked in the cage within the heart inside the locket. Instead, I live in my own fantasy world daily with real people, just different aptitudes, and I picture myself being happy, goofy, joyful and adored. There's not a day that I don't enter my fantasy world less than ten times a day. I get so much excitement when things go the way I plan/want them to go in my head. I've also learned that gospel music helps change my ungodly-like feelings into god-like ones. Yet when I stop, the same opiate feelings I don't want to feel find their way back in my heart and feel it all over again. In my head, as long as something was to happen to me, good or bad, it can or shall happen to me again. So, my mind is now programmed to expect it all again regardless of the situation.

Like someone was to start a brand-new relationship to an addiction of whatever drug you decide to use once you've received it, whether it was what you expected, your mind is still set up to continue receiving it regardless of what it is or was. Just like bills will forever be bills, it's the same way far as my feeling the way I felt growing up from a kid into an adult. I expect everything I've already experienced to go through it again so that I'm surprised, nor do I allow myself to get too comfortable. However, sometimes I still learn new things almost every day. Whether I was to repeat the same situation to learn a new lesson (apparently, I've done many times already) to going through a new situation, I'll still program it in my head that I'll go through it again, or it shall happen again so that I'm aware. So I've slowly become immune to death, depression, disappointment, surrounded by untrusted people with their disloyal ways, with the "I don't give a care" attitude. After I have put that in my head, thanks to the help of those around me, I've begun to see life for what it really is/can be/how it can end up being. It makes it no better when you realize no one is as real as I need them to be. Instead, they show fake love to one another and will get mad if you call them out on their fakeness. So instead of confronting people, I sit back and put in my mind that you can trust no one nor be loyal to them unless you're insane and want to feel and be hurt repeatedly, allowing others to hurt you continually.

It may seem mean, but in all actuality, mentally, you're simply just trying to protect yourself... with your heart in this case and prevent future problems. However, in my case and many others, no matter what we do, how we do it, trouble, complications, disappointment will take their chance to be in your life whether or not you invited them. Unfortunately, after trying so many times, I came to realize there's nothing you can do about it but ride it out like a gangstafied thug built to handle and conquer all.

Just like watching your child make mistakes repeatedly, no matter what you say or do to your child, the child will still make his/her own mistakes. You're left to watch it on the sidelines, although sometimes I force myself to be around others just to take a break from reality and realize how alone and unloved I really feel on the inside. Instead, I get them and myself high and talk mess since I have a smart/slick mouth, then go home to get higher just to face the best part of my day, which is sleep. My nightmares are better than my real life, especially the strange, creepy set dreams I have had in the past. People showed me, from my parents to my sex partners, that they all only show you attention just so they can use you for their own purposes. Once they get what they wanted from you, they couldn't care less about your feelings if you wanted/needed anything from them.

The book of Revelations says, "*Men will be in love with themselves*" and from what I've witnessed and been through in life, that part of the bible is accurate. For in today's world, people only care about themselves or simply put themselves before others regardless of who you are to them in their life, something God should have done when it comes to us and our disobedience toward Him and others, including ourselves. Some still care about their families, from aunts to uncles to cousins, while others only care about their friends and loved ones. Take it from me no one truly cares for me besides God Himself, my older brother and younger brother on my mom's side, and that one friend Fanny at this moment, but I still have my own back and am my own hero through God.

If the world let me see and realize that no one is for you nor cares about you but God, what should that tell you about yourself and how people really feel about you rather they were to tell you, show you, or if you're blind to it as I was blind to there at a point in time. My father's side of the family has love for me, but if I need anything from him and his people, from a place to rest my head to borrowing some money, I can't go to my dad or his family. I go to my Papa Toby for help. All he can offer is transportation just to throw it in your face and hold it over your head, so I slowly stop asking him for transportation. Still again, that's all he can offer due to the fact he puts his wife first, just like his youngest son and her wishes, as if I'm not his first grandchild or as if I have other people to depend on. Again, he's good for the few rides from time to time and will feed you if he has the money to do so. Still, that's not enough love for me to be satisfied, especially when he puts something over your head about the distance from my house to his house.

If my mom's mom were still alive, she would be the definition of loving others unconditionally, putting others before her, offering a helping hand when needed. If I were to need something/anything, I know she would have been there for me. Whether I was to have to learn a hard deflect lesson the hard way or not, I know I can count on her, and she'll never leave me nor forsake me and is the reason I'll mourn for her voice and touch every day for as long as I shall live. Don't get me wrong. I believe my family has love for me on both my parents' sides. However, if I needed them for anything, no one would ever be there for me, nor would I actually be around my family.

My mom's side of the family I've known since birth, yet not one member on that side of the family messed with me or my mom and her other three kids but watch how they will try to be in my life once I publish my first book. As far as my dad's side of the family goes, they show love, yet I feel like they don't fuck with me as well as I would love to mess with them. As far as my generation goes, I have love for all my cousins, and only a few show me love, including the ones that I talk to on Facebook, and the only time I was to see them is if I were to attend a party or invent of some sort. Even though we all as a family don't mess with each other as a whole, when we come together, we know how to have a good time, something my granny was good at doing whether or not each individual messed with you.

Still, however, that's not enough love for me to enjoy, cherish the life I'm currently living today, nor do I have a reason to wake up every morning. Instead, I'm just patiently waiting to die just so this lifetime can be over with, and in my eyes, as soon as I die, my life and everyone else's will be over with. Whatever happens after my life just will have to happen. Let it happen and pray that whatever happens next will be better than what I've already been through. Again, I realize what my heart yearns for I won't get until the next lifetime. So, as long as I live in this lifetime and whatever lifestyle I shall have, I'll never be completely satisfied, nor will I ever feel whole again especially living without my granny.

Looking and watching all the evil wickedness around me makes it no better how I feel on the inside and about this life/world we all have to live in. That same happy feeling I used to have and feel will come around again once God comes down and set the world and its people straight and shuts all the ungod-like people and ways down. Since I've near gotten my justice growing up, I feel like I'll never get my justice from my mom to my ex-best friend to the brain tumor. However, I'm convinced my justice will be delivered in due time through Christ Jesus when God gives His only begotten son the power/authority to lock Satan and his people with their wicked ways. Therefore, there will be no more evil, pain, betrayal, disloyalty, envy, and everything and anything that is not pleasing to God will be gone. Just like a broken relationship to food, once it's gone, it's not coming back. So yes, that's why I'm desperately waiting to die, not saying I want to experience it, but I can't wait until it's all over and so our God can see us through and enjoy life the way God Himself pictured us and get back to living on top of the world instead of living in the world. Until then, I'm stuck with my daily trials and tribulations that mess with my mind daily.

Unfortunately, I can blame no one for the trials but myself since I allowed it to consume my mind, and my mind does nothing but endure it all, whether good or bad memories. However, it seems like I have no control over it, nor can I tell my mind what to do or what not to do, yet my mind tells my body what to do, how to do it, what it feels, what it thinks it wants and much more. Imagine you now living off my mind and heart based on what I've told you so far. How would you yourself look at life after you've felt what I felt, seen what I've seen, and heard what I've heard? Would you become like me and have trust, abandonment, or neglected issues? Would you be like me and show others how happy you wish you could be? Would you continue to help others or give up hope in helping them at all? Most importantly, would you still believe in God and trust in him?

There's no need to actually answer these questions since I know my past was designed for me to walk down and is only fit for me and me only. Just like whoever's reading this book, your life is set up for you and only you and was made for you to walk down in their own unique way. If I had another life/path/story to tell, I wouldn't be the person I need/am today or become the person I shall be when my death approaches me. For again, I'm not right until I'm right with God. Try to understand what your mind is telling you or trying to tell you. Realize how you really feel about life as well as the situation you are currently in. Dig deep in your mind and discover all that you thought, wondered, could have known/felt. You'll be surprised by what you'll discover and produce. Again, take it from a person who has all day to let her mind run and run miles and miles deep inside. Not only does your mind control your body but also your thoughts, actions, and decision-making. Both your mind and heart control your body while the soul is there to witness it all.

Honestly, to keep it a hundred with you'll, God again knows what the mind is for, and I believe it's for our own good not to know everything about the mind and what it can do as of yet. I'm not saying He made a mistake, yet since Eve made the first mistake, we fail to know what the whole mind is capable of, so I believe God intervened, knowing how the world will turn out to be as we live in today's life and witness. Think about some of the very knowledgeable people and how crazy they sound rather than solving a math equation that is simple to them to the many strange ideas popping in your head. I feel the more we know of the mind/or a realization of it, the crazier people can seem to those who don't understand their own minds, let alone the next person. For example, people think I'm crazy because of my actions to my thoughts when I'm mad or troubled in any way possible. Before I do the troubled actions/words/feelings of a madman, my mind first consumes everything that it has been exposed to and based on the information received to the mind. It triggers my body to act/say upon the feeling of my heart and what the mind knows. Just like I can be given a lesson in school and a test at the end of the week to see if I passed, remembering the lesson taught to me is the exact way people show you that they're going to show you pain from disloyalty to betrayal. You began to feel hurt, angry, loveless, unimportant, low at times as if you're depressed, so the action is to avoid the past feelings and thoughts to come and retake their course in the future. The significant part of the life lesson is not to repeat the same mistakes and lessons and not to fold from it all. You may bend, but do not fold.

"Things change, rearrange and so do I, it isn't always for the good drag I can't lie, I get high 'cause the road can be so cold, I may bend a little, but I won't fold, if you see my tears fall just let me be, move along there's nothing to see," quoted by Cole.

I've repeated the same mistakes in the past, but once I realized the pattern, I put a stop to it and changed some things. If you fail at this point, it's like failing the whole test in grade school and having to repeat it in order to exceed the next grade level. The only difference is if you or I were to let our minds continue to feel the way it does now and allow room for more or similar feelings/ emotions to enter, not only will I become insane, but I will self-destruct, and that's what makes a person go crazy. That's why I smoke weed and get high to cope with life and its effects. Besides that, prayer itself and listening to gospel music from Yolanda Adams, "Never Give Up, I'm Going To Be Ready, And I Got To Believe" (in that order) to my dude Kirk Franklin just to ease my mind. It's hurt and pain, and its many emotions, and if I weren't to go to them three things, I too would become crazier than Hitler himself.

I won't lie. It's hard, but it helps to think about God and his promise that will soon come to pass, and truth be told, I can't wait for that promise to be fulfilled. I also still think about how my life could have been if I never had the brain tumor or how I will have the use of my right hand and foot since I was born with a fully functional body. I wonder if I would be close to the same person as I am today. Definitely not, and God Himself can generate both you and I that. Let's just say God knows how to get someone's undivided attention that will make that person pay attention whether the person wanted to or not. Again, I said God led me down this crooked path so my soul can become the spirit God originally put in me as well as see in me, for I yet not see what God sees in me. I need His will given to me through him to be done, and it shall be done in Jesus' name. Amen.

How Life Could Have Been If I Weren't Disabled

Let's just say this life that I lived as a kid was the exact way, minus my disability. My entire life would have been different for sure had I never had that stupid brain tumor, the seizures, the sudden halt in the beating of my heart, and being pronounced dead after five minutes of no movement. Thank you, God, for my granny's prayers that it wasn't my time to die, although I'd rather have dealt with my death back then as an infant than later in the future. Back to the point, let's just say everything in my life went the same way, from my first fight to my granny and her family's death to the way my mom treated me as a kid, to the day my older brother left me to deal with my mom and her b.s. for starters.

After years of praying, surviving, the pain and the hurt, the situation, the starvation, I went through it okay without my brother, Tez, going through it with me. Not only did we understand each other, but we felt the same pain, yet he took no b.s. from no one when it came to me. Tez made me feel powerful yet protected, and by him being a male and watching him grow up, he was my male role model, and everything he did I had to do, and as long as he was with me doing it, I was cool, regardless of what situation we were in. However, the day he left and went to stay with our Uncle Spunky was the beginning of his freedom along with Mookie, Cash, Scooter, and Spunky had, so in my eyes, my life was now fucked.

It changed within the first five minutes after Tez left. I had to get to cleaning, and I was now the only one cleaning the house, besides the dishes, which my mom did to the grass getting cut. However, a girl still had to shovel, so I probably for sure would do it all by myself, including the dishes plus the yard if it wasn't for God allowing me to become disabled. I would have happily gone to Kennedy High School. However, I doubt I would have gotten into the two fights I did during the three months there. Then again, I know I would have probably fought a couple of fights being the angry kid I was growing up, which is not taking any b.s. from anyone regardless of who you were.

Imagine if I were to fight with both my hands instead of the one hand I have. People say I can fight with the one hand I have, and I know I can with my one hand thanks to the play fights I had in the past and my granny telling me to get out there and fight, so imagine me doing it with two how worse it could have gotten. I would have a different group of fake friends and still meet up with the old ones from elementary years and possibly fight. Knowing my tolerance level and mouth, I still would have gone to LuraWood and Cleveland Clinic again on the sixth floor in the crazy hospital, plus still going to jail at Lincoln Place in Youngstown, Ohio.

Still, within the three short months, I was at Kennedy, my tenth-grade year. I would have been easily talked into having sex, sleeping with who knows what, and nine times out of ten, more than half of whomever I was to sleep with, I would be using them for something I watched

Tez do growing up to his many female friends. I would have been in a relationship. However, in my reality, I've never been faithful to my boyfriends, so it would have probably been the same way for my personal excuse and reasons I was to do it in the first place. My little reputation would have been slightly different until the time I was kicked out and sent back to my first high school, Hope High, after the multiple trouble I was in being at Hope High school around my brother Tez with his niggas and the many girls who wanted to have sex with him. My reputation was affected there, from my fights to boyfriends to the different groups of fake friends. However, at that school, I was Tez's shadow, and my class, both upper and lower class, knew me as Tez's little sister, and I was always his shadow in any school we were to attend.

The only thing that would have been different with school life was the fights. Half of the fights I've fought, I believe I wouldn't have had to fight since most of the fights were based on underestimating me because of my hand. People always assumed I was weak, making assumptions due to my disadvantage. I fought as a kid to prove my point that I'm far from weak/disabled, thanks to my granny telling me to get out there and fight. Otherwise, the who I would have fought back then would be different, so returning to Hope High School, I would have picked up where I left off. Since school was the only freedom I had at the time, I would take advantage of it all, from skipping school to having sex with God knows who to smoking and drinking to acting the way I used to act in school, still shutting our high school down from being in gangs and riots 24/7. Since I was already on probation and already attended Daily Report Program, I would have still gone to jail, and only God knows how many times I would have gone there, especially while my mom was/ is until this day.

The best part about that is if I were to do the things I did, from going to Kid Health 20/20 to my probation appointments and doing what I had to do, I would have been cool staying out of the house practicing for the OGT test. I probably would have failed the test and not even cared to take it nor pass it since my hope, ambition, strive (my brother was my motivation) was gone and staying was hard/hell on earth, and I would have felt the same way my little sister Tink is feeling right now since I'm now watching her go through the same b.s. Tez and I went through during the once in a blue moon that I would go over to my mom's house. It's not the memories I get, but the vibes and the negative emotions felt at the time.

Let's just say my summer of 2007 went the same way, and I went to South High School, which I really didn't want to go to. I'm confident I would have gotten into fights since my mouth is reckless, and I was a new face to a new territory staining on the east side of Cleveland, Ohio, especially since I only knew a handful of people. Since I'm not around the down the way area, I feel people would have tried me, and I would have given them what they wanted plus the sex, skipping school, drinking, and getting high, and I would have had a different group of friends. My ex-BFF Meka may or may not have been my ex-best friend, and I still would have tried to take the OGT test whether I passed or failed. On the strength that all who attended Hope

High transcripts were lost, we all had to take it again, but still, I would have passed or not if I had been encouraged enough to retake it. My mind was set that the only way out of the hell life I had was through school and school only. If I passed the OGT test, I would take the opportunity to further my education in college along with the setbacks and mistakes. If I didn't pass it, let's just say plan b to survive and get out of my mom's hell house will slowly reveal itself momentarily, later on in this book.

As far as my days attending South High School, only God knows in detail how it would have happened and how I would have been acting during that time. My reputation would have been slightly different, but my attitude, personality, and behavior would have been the same. I was simply suffering from the past hurt, pain, neglect, carelessness, feeling unloved, loneliness, feeling like a slave, hating life, still committing suicide, still on probation, and home detention to house arrest. On top of all that, I would have still gone to jail for the many things my mom claims I did, from throwing a book in her face to threatening her with a knife saying, *"Bitch, I'll kill you,"* which was all a lie. I still would have spent Christmas and the other holidays in jail, and I probably would have wild out like a loose animal not under control or would have been kissing ass and took it as the vacation from the house and the b.s. my mom put me through. However it would have played out, I still would look at it as a break/vacation from my reality. It is a messed-up way, but it would have felt good and relieved to finally get some peace. I would have sucked all the freedom (in my eyes) that was there even though it's not a comfortable place to live, but it felt better to be in jail with the other young people than living my life with my mom behind closed doors.

Now again, if I passed the five parts of my OGT, I would have taken the ACT or SAT, but if I knew I failed, I would have never taken the ACT or SAT I initially took in 2009. The summer of 2008 would have gone the same from having a job, being on house arrest, going to Cincinnati, going to Kings Island, getting drunk with my dad and one of his many female friends to still kicking it with Ms.

Trouble, possibly Meka and her cousins and brothers, being bothered by my mom and her ways. During the short time that Tez came to town to visit, my summer of 2009 would have played out the same way, from the different jobs to seeing my cousins to dealing with my mom and different fake friends. By then, I would have had or come up with a plan to leave my mom's house as soon as I was eighteen and done with high school.

If I were going off to college, I would stay on campus in the dorms as a place to stay and be on a meal plan. Because my school used my financial aid for college, whatever college I was to go to, I would have completed a semester after high school along with the course I took in high school going to Bryant and Stratton College. However, if I didn't pass the OGT, I would look for a job to earn income and maintain shelter, yet it shouldn't have been that difficult to find employment. Still, only God knows, and I'm confident I would have found a job since I worked at Cedar Point before and during my senior year in high school before I quit if I had quit after Tez and I were working there. Nine times out of ten, I would have worked and saved money until after Halloween.

Of course, my mom's hand would have been out, but I would have taken any and every chance I had of my mom's absence any day. As long as she wasn't in the picture, I was cool, and I would have been cool being someone's employee working, stacking, and finding a way out of the hell house I was living in at the time. The year 2010, however, would have been different in so many ways. And I'm about to break it all down starting in March 2010, going through it with my mom.

Whether I walked the stage, I still would have signed up to work at Cedar Point at my brother Tez. The sweet deal of that plan was that as soon as I got the notice to go work back at Cedar Point, I would have never cared to walk the stage on June 6, 2010, knowing what I'd been through. Me losing my high school diploma, I never even would have attempted to walk the stage, especially since Cedar Point was open already waiting for college regardless if I was attending it or not. I would work weekend shifts since I was now eighteen, and as soon as I was done with school, Sandusky, Ohio would be my next destination. So by my work history and plans for the future, I would have worked at Cedar Point, working, saving, having a place to stay, food to eat, possibly looking forward to college up until I was in my current debt as of 2015.

So by, three times after graduation, I would have been away from my mom (hell house), but first, I had to get through March to May, and that time was hard. During that time, things slowly changed for the worse. If I didn't pass the OGT test, I knew I wouldn't graduate, and like Tez, I still would have taken the opportunity to go to Cedar Point. And I would have enjoyed the time there better than the time I would have been at my mom's house, but first again, I have to get through March to get to May. Long story short, and for those who read my book (*Behind Every Smile*), both you and I are witnesses to how my mom treated me, still getting kicked out of her house as if I weren't paying rent. I would go over to Mz. Trouble's house frequently if I had to. If not there, I went over to my other friend's house, Neice, who, at the time, stayed down the street from me. I would have been more comfortable staying over at Mz. Trouble's house, knowing what type of house she lived in and what type of freedom I thought I had or how it was in my eyes.

As many times as I went to school from Mz. Trouble's, I would have moved into her house without second-guessing it, especially after the last time I went to jail for something I didn't do. Plus, when I pushed Boogie off the porch after he started the whole drama by lying on me and getting told to hit me, thanks to my mom making matters worse and knowing how my mom is, she called the police. Since I was just there to grab some clothes and spend a few days wherever my fake friend Nikki was going to sleep at night, I instead went to jail.

However, it would have played out. I would have stayed and moved in with Mz Trouble being exposed to drugs, the pricing out of selling drugs, weed, pills, watching people cook crack in a microwave using a baby food jar, and much more. It's just like being in a typical trap house. Thanks to Mz. Trouble and watching her friends gave me the idea of sleeping with guys for money, I slowly got the hang of it. Plus, my version of freedom, highness, and food, and since I love sex... I would have lived the fast, fun life of getting money, getting the idea to be like my role model Tez and selling stuff with Mz. Trouble's boyfriend at the time and his people, all for the money and the money only.

I was simply money-hungry, and since I couldn't/didn't have any of my own plate, I was going to try to eat and not starve. Plus, I watched my mom financially struggle while physically changing, and I didn't want to become like her in that situation. Plus niggas are nothing, so I knew what to do, and being like both Tez and my dad, it wasn't hard. I would have also stopped praying and talking to God because the lack of faith was getting dried up as the days were to pass me by, and once I was getting what I've wanted and prayed for far as living and finally experienced how to live a life as a kid, better yet a teenager. By my version of freedom, I would have finally arrived and again stopped praying to God since I thought there was no need to continue to pray. I thought this was the way out, and in my mind, we would be set on getting money and getting my own whether or not I was to graduate school.

However, March would have gone, it would have come to pass, and April was no better in my eyes. As soon as May would have hit, I would be back at Cedar Point regardless of how much fun I would have had. That was a good opportunity to stay out there, work, eat, get money, and since Tez was out there, I looked up to him and felt safe and motivated around him. Both he and I have a mindset that was forced on us by our mom, which was to get money and never become broke. There are pros and cons to my mom's daily trouble, b.s., and drama. We're just animals trying to survive by any means necessary when it comes to living in my mom's house.

So back to if I were to graduate and head off to college, I would have gone through the summer of 2010 not meeting Meka's neighborhood friends from Cliff, to Nitty, to Tev to Kid, and I wish I only met Nitty. I would have never met Rae (Meka's friend) nor spent my summer over Meka's people's house, nor Niece still waiting until August to go to school. Instead, I would have been working at Cedar Point, enjoying all it offered from money to half price on everything — riding the roller coasters at the theme park for free when I'm off to the many parties they help for their employees. I would have partied hard with my brother and other co-workers stacking money for college, and the best part about it was the fact I was with my brother, the person I went through everything with from birth.

There's nothing like a bond between two siblings, especially with an older brother. Since his mission is to protect me by any means necessary, including his other two siblings, nothing or no one can come between that. No matter how many times we fall out, we're still all we have.

Since we miss our granny, we each imagine her being in the midst of our lives since we all are a part of her. Thanks to my mom, we all were connected to my granny at a point in time in the past. Since we didn't have my mom the way we needed to have her, we were left with each other along with our two younger siblings once they got a taste of life as we saw it in today's world.

If I weren't to graduate and go off to college, I would have had two options. One would be to link up with my brother Tez and be involved with him and his way of living life. I would have taken the same road he took since he left Cedar Point with his wrong of a girlfriend, Lex. I wouldn't have wanted to stay around, for he, too, has a story of his own that should be told. Then again, most of us have a story, situation, shared experience that changed them that they can never go back from to the old them and ways even if they really desired to.

The other option I would have had was to link back up with Mz. Trouble knowing the type of lifestyle she was living and being back in the trap house that was quite fun to live/beat but not to stay and die at. Especially if I was fed up with my brother and the different route he has taken, including going to jail, to selling drugs, to killing people, seeing people die, being out in the streets, abandoned houses, around untrustworthy friends, both job hiring and job losing, and becoming enslaved to Lex filling the role of my mom in Tez's life. She took/is taking care of him since we both fear being and live alone, yet I'm facing it by myself as I write this book.

Since I wasn't graduating, going to college, or having future plans to survive, I know I would have made the same mistake moving back in with Mz. Trouble not wanting to deal with my brother and his drama. Then my life would have slowly gone downhill, but before I say more, I must have you imagine my life, which is the purpose of this section in this book, for I need you to understand me, my situations, and circumstances.

Now let's say I walked the stage starting from attending Bryant and Stratton College, taking the course of criminal justice for the justice part (something I had a problem with receiving ever since my granny died to my surgery). I would have then gone to a school close to Cedar Point and was planning on making easy money, saving it just to use it for future reasons from living since I wasn't trying to return to my mom's house no matter what was to happen to me. As of the summer, I would have stayed on campus during my work at the job. I then would have gone straight to school, living off my financial aid plus the money I've saved from working at Cedar Point. So as soon as school had started, I would have entered college life with what I experienced with my mom treating me wrongly, to staying with Mz. Trouble's in high school getting exposed to the trap house b.s. to having the experience of Cedar Point. I would have added all I went through to college life, and my mind/goal will be set on money, school, shelter, food, weed in that order.

So ask yourself, what will you do with a mindset to hustle, use people, smoke weed, sell maybe drugs depending on Coco's product and the people I was to deal with selling pussy I learned from Mz. Trouble friend Cyn plus the mindset to get money. Besides focusing on money and ways to get it legal or illegal, I would be focused on school, work, and assuming everything would go just fine, thinking my financial aid would cover my following two semesters from the classes to the dorms. I would have had the money for food and my books. If possible, I would have gone to college, set myself up to work at a part-time job, sell pussy, weed, drugs, do my schoolwork, and spend money, but not all, plus I had to leave campus on holidays.

Still, with the same mindset of taking no b.s. from no one, I could have still possibly fault other college students, or I might not, and my group of friends would have been different. I would have also visited Cleveland to see my old fake friends and keep in contact with my mom, brother, possibly Mz. Trouble and Meka and was building a new reputation. With the small dose of college life I experienced, I enjoyed being exposed to a society full of different people from all over the world with different backgrounds.

Before I say more, the purpose of this book is to let my readers, especially those who came from a different background or getting cut from a different cloth, meaning you guys have a different, more fortunate lifestyle. Some come from families who are wealthy or could come from a family who help and support one another the best way they know how or to the orphan who doesn't even know their families to people who've been in and out of the adoption system hiding what they really felt on the inside, to families who have been raped, molested, bullied on, abused both mentally and physically, or sexually to my kind of family which is an "every man for themselves" type system being out in the world alone and only for you and to only count on you and your family just stopped fucking with you for their reasons.

All that in one state left alone earth and as each person you ever cross paths with or see, you'll never know who they are, where they came from, what they went/go through, and were they trying to head in life. We simply fail to understand someone simply by the lack of love we share with one another. We ignore others but our own worlds we live in and all we have been exposed to, whether good or bad, rich or poor. The majority only care about things based on what they know, what was said to them, exposed, adjusted to in life. Regardless of the role in their life, we couldn't care less about all that we don't know. My job/what I'm trying to do is open up the eyes of those who don't/can't see nor feel how people with scars, tears, bruises, damaged acts or feels, and it's those who require help while others who don't feel, hear, see what others see, feel and hear, for again we couldn't care less of what we fail to realize and understand.

Getting back to the story, if I were using what I knew I had plus attended school, everything would have seemed cool until winter break took its course. Whether I was to go off to college, my life still would have changed for the worse, and I firmly believed that God allowed me to become disabled just to save me from self-destruction and becoming faithless.

As soon as the second week of December in 2010 came around, I would have been notified that I didn't have enough financial aid to continue next semester (since we had all been in some type of debt before). And since I already had a debt taking out a loan for my first semester, I would have failed to schedule classes for next semester, so instead, I would have to find a new place to rest my head. I probably would have given Tez another chance, staying with him wherever he was before looking for other options. I would have had to drop out of school until I could pay back my student loan. So either way, on how my life would have started, I would have still had to leave college no matter how long I stayed there, and my primary focus would be on finding and maintaining shelter for myself.

So now, as I ended the year 2010, I would have been searching for a house. Whether I was to have a job in Akron, Ohio, I eventually would have given my brother another chance and still be exposed to Tez's lifestyle and messed-up situations. I would only be worried about and doing me from selling pussy and knowing my brother, and what he's about and do, I'd be selling drugs and weed. I'd be making money, saving money, and on my way back to working at Cedar Point. Whether I was to have a job or not, I would spend the summer of 2011 working at Cedar Point, stacking money as I go. The best part is that I would have had my brother right there by my side.

Again only God knows details on what I would actually do. I have a clue that I will be selling what I can sell, just like my mom taught her kids, from weed to pussy, using guys just to hustle and get money paying back my loan so I can focus on returning to college at the same time getting high, drunk, partying, turning up. I would have never considered coming back to Cleveland, Ohio, basically because of my mom and my past. I would have made the majority of the money that I've saved from either working if I had a job. If not, I would have just saved up the money I earned from working at Cedar Point in 2011 and worked on paying my loan off, not to mention still being on probation until August 16th, 2011.

Now let's say I didn't want to stay with my brother and his many situations again, me staying with Mz. Trouble would have been the person to start a foundation with after leaving Cedar Point the day after Halloween of 2011. My experience would have been the same way it initially did in 2011 (for those who read my book *Walking Testimony* should know how that lifestyle of mine went). Hopefully, you should now have a clear picture of how I would be starting my life.

Whether I was to graduate and go off to college, I still would have had the same mindset to selling pussy and weed to using guys, saving money, working if I had a job. If I didn't, I would be simply waiting to work at Cedar Point again, but my mind would be most focused on finding and maintaining a place I could call home, regardless of who I was to stay with. It would have been too real since I needed some type of income from having a place to stay, paying for personals, clothing, and food. Whether I graduated high school or dropped out, I would have gone through 2010 and 2011, staying with my brother or Mz. Trouble, but my mentality, mindset, feelings would have remained the same. The only difference would be the fake friends I would chill with to the boys I slept with. I would have been on probation, knowing I was desperate to get out of the justice system and going back and forth to court for domestic violence charges. I didn't need to be developing a reputation of that nature as I was becoming a young adult being nineteen going on twenty.

Still, whatever path I was to take both years (2010, 2011) would have ended the same way it started. However it went down, I would have still worked at Cedar Point, and after that, my life could have gone elsewhere. I would have saved my money from Cedar Point, completed my probation, and as soon as I was to get off, I would have felt free. As soon as I was done working at Cedar Point, I would have decided where I would rest my head, whether with my brother back with Mz. Trouble or finding my own spot. Honestly, from what I know now and compared it to what I would have known/ should have known, if I still went through what I originally went through in my life, I would have probably moved back in with Mz. Trouble in November 2011. If not getting the hours on Griffin Street with either Mz. Trouble or Dai-day slow self.

Either way, I would have gotten that place for six months staying in Cleveland. Even if I were with Tez and his b.s., I still would have stayed wherever I was to stay for six months. Only God knows what would have initially happened in those six months until working back at Cedar Point since it was the coolest, most enjoyable job I've ever experienced so far. The question would be, how would the next six months from November 2011 until April 2012 play out? I do know I would have had a place to stay, and the only thing on my mind would be how to maintain more income, pay rent and bills and still pay off my student loan (if I walked the stage), and since I'm not disabled, I wouldn't have a check to survive. That means I have to use what I already got to get what I need/want — money. In other words, getting to sell my pussy and knowing the knowledge of living and being in the trap house selling drugs would have been another means for income, especially if I was to still hang with Mz. Trouble and her friends. Watching her friends alone would have inspired me to become a stripper and sell pussy along with the weed and drugs just to make money. I probably would be doing/taking drugs just out of curiosity and would not have cared about the reputation I was now building, not caring who knew what.

Did you realize how God isn't in the pictures, my dreams, or my plans? Did you wonder how little faith I would have for him down to the lack of hope, trust, love, and prayer? I would have honestly forgotten about God forsaking him, giving up on him since I felt my previous prayers were never answered. Since he never saved me from what I experienced growing up with my mom, I would have slowly begun living IN the world instead of living OF the world. My morals, values, and self-respect would have been all over the place, and the year would have been fun for the flesh but not of the spirit, for my spirit inside would have still died.

Ending 2011, I was trying to decide whether I was to stay with Mz. Trouble or my brother, I would be doing the same thing I initially did (for those who read my second book, *Walking Testimony,* you're familiar with how my brother will let me use a guy for money that I used to buy weed to get me and him high, especially since I didn't have to sleep with every guy I ever used). In my real life, I still will have the same mindset as I have right now as I write this book. It goes like this... get money, trust no one, fuck this world, use niggas, survive, maintain shelter, and the love for my siblings would have been the same.

By 2012, I would have still slowly stopped chilling with Mz. Trouble since I knew what type of person she was, plus I knew what road she was heading down, meaning depending on others, using others, becoming lazy to help herself. The days of living together would have been figuring out what type of person she really is. Mz. Trouble is the actual definition of a fuck nags, for she would do what she has to do to get what she's trying to get, not caring whom she has to cross and hurt and stab in the back. Of course, I would have followed my brother wherever he was to go. Yet, my goal would have been to get my own and work from the bottom, having every dream a true hustler has, which is to get to the top of the pyramid by any means necessary, and honestly, I believe finding God wouldn't be a part of my agenda. I would have stopped praying trusting, and my faith would have no longer been there.

Don't get me wrong. I still consider myself saved, for I believe God created Jesus Christ, who he sent down to die on the cross for my sins to be forgiven by God, and he was, is, and will always be my personal Lord and Savior and only through him I shall be saved. However, if I were living life without my disability, I would have known that there is a God being raised in the church. Yet, my lack of faith and trust toward Him would have taken its course, and again I would have given up on God, believing he gave up on me and my many prayers. Would I be like those who don't believe in God? I highly doubt that, but the devil was going to have an open invitation to my life and should do all his lustful desires for the love of money. I would have self-destructed for Satan himself comes to kill, steal, and destroy, and I was doing all three.

I would definitely be stealing, taking advantage of others, using people. I would be killing my soul, for it will no longer be of good use if I were to continue to use it harmfully, giving in to Satan who has all power of death since all sins lead to death, and he himself was the first to commit sin, which is jealousy, one of the seven deadly sins. I would be destroying myself, my belief, mind, value, respect, faith, etc.

The year 2012 would have been about drugs, money, using others, and gaining a reputation that would follow me wherever I go. Sex would have slowly taken its course and role since I have to admit I like it too much, and through that, I would be blind to what life is really about. I would have neither dealt with my family on both my parents' side of their families. The only good thing about this fantasy dream is that I would have never gone through the situation I went through with my brother and lost everything I ever owned but three outfits thanks to the b.s. Tez was in that month of May.

Another good thing is I would never have been in the fights I was in from Big B and her biting me, and me biting her back tasting her skin in my teeth to the fight with Nikki and my dislocation of the shoulder. Afterward, the fallout with Shorty (more details in *Walking Testimony*) and her stealing from me to the niggas I fucked and the friends I chilled with would have been different. I still would have made an appearance to my mom's mother's side of the family, who don't mess with me yet show off the fake love they be trying to give me. I would have still cried like my granny was there since all her kids were there, minus one kid who died at birth, and all her grandkids were there but two. Yet, no one saw or paid attention to her presence, but me, and that's what made me burst out crying, plus the fact of how distant we are toward one another from my aunty who touched me to my little uncle to my mom. Of course, I would have shown up with my brother, got high, checked in at a hotel that night, and the next day would have gone back to the real life of hustling, getting high, and maintaining money.

Knowing Tez and his hopping around from state to state every three months, who knows where I would be technically staying at the time, but a girl would have had her a house stripping, selling weed, drugs, and pussy, using random guys for money and weed. I was going to feel satisfied with my life and how I was living it. I couldn't have asked for anything else. The year 2012 would have begun and ended partying, getting high using people and all about my siblings and me, and I would have started the year 2013 just the same way. I still would have been working at Cedar Point, stacking my money, and possibly looking for a permanent job. Then again, messing with my brother and his different moves, I probably would have never kept a permanent job, especially if I was never to graduate.

Back to my other life. Had I graduated and dropped out of college, I would have searched for employment. If hired, I would work, pay taxes, sell weed, pussy, and drugs for extra income, use guys, strip when needed, and aim to go back to college only this time I would attend a community college before Obama was to be out of office. You best believe I would have been saving my money to pay off my student loans and go to school by 2014 using my financial aid. This time I would have attended a community college of my choice, doing college a little differently, knowing and realizing my mistakes the first time around.

On the strength that I adored college life and always thought that the way out the hood, ghetto, slums and the bottom of the pyramid was through school, I would have had a little motivation to use the education system just to gain knowledge on how to help other kids who lives were like mine. I would want to help them get the justice they deserve before the children let their past lives mess them up mentally. That dream goal never changed since I went to jail for something I never did nor will ever do to my mother regardless of what she's done to me. Sadly, that record follows me today as I write this book having a domestic violence (DV) charge, which she has on three of four of her kids.

Either way, with how my life could have gone, whether with school or without school up until the year of 2013, we all know the common denominator in this lifestyle of minds with the same dreams/goals, just different paths. Especially if I were to never have had my many shoulder dislocations in 2012, I would have been cool on the body side, having no surgery. I would have kept my body in shape, and as conceited as I am, I would do the walk and talk of a conceited female sharking at people, regardless of the relationship status. I would have been the new and improved Jezebel and not ashamed of it.

The year 2013 would have been the same (more details in *Walking Testimony*) minus the different fake friends I would have and sex toys/partners. There would have never been a fall out with my ex-best friend Meka and me to her breaking into my house taking everything I owned, causing me to start over with the outfit on my back, plus an outfit I had to attend a wedding I couldn't care less about, the same b.s. I went through with my brother just a year before. My and my mother's relationship still wouldn't be on good terms but not as bad as it is now, and how she played a part in the beginning when Meka and I fell out to Meka breaking into my house. If only my mom did something different, like being real for a change and stopping with the pointless unnecessary b.s. she likes to start. My brother and I would have never gotten into an argument beefing over his girlfriend, which my mom again had everything to do with, just like she always did between my brother and me since we were kids. I would have definitely never gone through surgery on my left arm. I would have never even suffered from another shoulder dislocation ten weeks after my first surgery, thanks to a guy hitting me with a wooden stick, causing my shoulder to fall out of socket messing around with Mz. Troubler and her bestie Mek-Mek.

What still would have happened regardless of what lifestyle I was to live was the death of my great aunt, and I still would have missed her funeral thanks to my mom not telling me anything about it. My number one papa and two other males from both sides of my family died within the last week of May in 2013. The difference is that instead of going to all three funerals that I originally went to in three days, I would have only gone to my number one papa, of course. Since I didn't know my cousin personally, I would have never gone to him. Since I didn't meet my dad's side of the family until I was fifteen, I would have never cared to be bothered with them since they weren't in the picture from the beginning, knowing they should have been there from the start.

My Papa Toby and my dad, Special, I would have kept up with from time to time. If I were with Tez, I would have never gone there or dealt with them or gotten to know my family members I initially met at the funeral to the many parties Papa Toby had. So I would have missed my great papa's funeral. Then again, I probably would have gone showing up to the party both before and after the funeral on the strength that my number one papa funeral was two days before my great papa's funeral was. However, that would have played out, it would have come to pass, and by September 2013, my mom would have still kicked my little sister Tink out of the house, and by Tez or me not being in town to get there, I don't know what would have happened, only God knows. Technically I would, by all means, get Tink to a safe place knowing she was outside walking the streets of Kinsman, which is the east side of Cleveland where people from my older cousin Murddy (long live Murddy) to a three-month-old baby just two streets away from where my mom stay let alone on all up in down the strip of Kinsman. So again, only God Himself really knows what would've really happened to Tink.

I can imagine Tez and me getting our sister. Knowing the initial situation that we all had to deal with as far as dealing with our mom and for those who read my second book knows how she was out the home for three days until my mom finally called the police, bringing them to my house as if I was going to open up the door. However, that would have gone far as the situation with my sister getting kicked out of the house would have still played out. The only good thing about 2013 was no surgery, plus no shoulder dislocations. Nor will I have experienced my ex-best friend breaking into my house taking everything I ever owned from food to clothes, to household items to my number one papa obituary, let alone the other obituaries, which she burned in my tub.

As of 2015, as I write this book, I still see the burn marks in my tub every time I was to take a shower. Meka took everything, including my furniture, shoes, blinds, shower curtains, my cable cord to my clothes. She gave all my stuff to my fake neighbors in the building, plus left my door wide open for the people who stay on 55th to take everything down to my cable box to my railing to my bed, and the only thing they left was my mattress. Meka and her dumb, immature cousin took the batteries out of my remote to the dirty bed bug couch they brought in my house that came from only God knows where. However, I think it came from the trash/dumpster. They even wiped their asses with my toothbrush.

That plus the dislocation of my shoulder were the two worse pains I felt, besides the death of my number one papa and the fact that I owed him ten dollars for helping me move in my third house, but I never paid him back. I could have avoided all of what I was experiencing with communication and understanding. The real reason I went to the wedding was to get paid to babysit and used that money plus the rest of the money I had in November to buy two pairs of joggings pants, five shirts, plus five more pairs of pants I got from who know where, and a few more shirts. I made it all last until the day after Thanksgiving when I got my SSI check unexpectedly on that day, and my Papa Toby told me about it.

God saw me through after suffering for two weeks, feeling miserable, but within the two months, almost after God blessed me with a house full with three couches, a recliner, two beds, two tables, food, almost twenty outfits, and boots for the winter. God really showed up and showed out. He'll work in ways you fail to imagine until it happens, and God knows I love to shop for newer things, and that's what I've done my whole 2014 — buying bottles and getting high. However, if I went into my other fantasy life, I imagine not only would I miss the opportunity for God to show up and out, but God and I would have never had the relationship we do now. For through my pain, I've seen him. That's another reason for this book. It's proof that God makes no mistake because, again, I'm going to paint a picture of how my life could have gone out up until 2015.

My vision of life versus God's Will for my life would have never met the way it needed to be met.

Back to my fantasy life again. I would have gone through 2014 the same way as the previous years, from partying to working at Cedar Point to hustling money and still stacking and maintaining to keep money. If I were to go to school, I would have paid my twenty-two hundred attending a community college if I hadn't tried to do it in 2013. I would have a permanent place to stay, and 2014 would be my year going back to school for sure just to afford a decent lifestyle. If Meka didn't set me back, I would have attended college in the winter of 2016, starting where I left off, refreshing my memory of what I need to know to do what I have to do to get what I wanted/needed.

Again, if I didn't get my high school diploma, college would be out of the equation, especially if I never passed a GED test. If I were motivated to take it and if I were to pass, then I would go off to college. However, if I didn't pass the test, there would be no college for me.

Therefore, following my dreams to dedicate my life to others get their justice to helping all kids in teens who are in any type of crisis from child abuse mentally, physically, or emotionally. I want to become a counselor who helps families with the petty problems they take for granted. That's the purpose of helping those children in their family who need consoling, love, grace, and forgiveness and help get rid of the pain and need help not to destroy their lives. God blessed us all with whack we'll never be worthy of, yet however, love conquers all, and God means that.

Anyway, if I were living my fantasy life, I would either be in school, still hustling, when needed and possibly have a job, and that would be my spring and fall semester working on a dream my mom sowed in me and is still my dream as I write this book. If I were to walk the stage, I would only simply look forward to working at Cedar Point and stacking money, afraid to lose it all and to work to get more money. Besides money, I would be heavy on weed and sex since I love all three. I will be lusting all the wrong things, sin after sin that only God Himself knows how he would have felt for me. Plus, my judgment day would be a five thousand bible rep sheet long, and I would have had an express ticket sending me straight with a gasoline spirit.

No matter how art I believed in God, my heart would have been IN the world around its evil and wicked ways, and my heart would never be ON God but more toward the devil and his evil ways. The only good thing about this life is that Tink would have never been over Momma T's house, which only God Himself knows what really went down in that house. She would still have been kicked out of the house, but maybe her dad would have dealt with that situation by then... maybe. Again, only God knows how that would have played out in the end. My mom's mom's father's family reunion in 2014, I wouldn't have cared less to attend. I definitely wouldn't be around my dad's side of the family, for the ones I included as members of my dad's fantasy family. However, I would have gone to the family reunion they had in 2015, but that's it.

The ending of 2014 would have ended with me partying and doing things that made me feel happy. If I graduated, I would start 2015 in my fifth semester. Hopefully, I would have finally walked the path with the same mindset and agenda, down to the bad habits such as having sex for money, using people, selling weed to dog food, and other drugs. If possible, while doing that, schoolwork, study, and job, I would simply do what Kristelle really felt like doing no matter who cared about what and who felt any type of way point-blank. If I weren't looking forward to school, I would be doing the same thing I've been doing since high school. I'm just smarter, wiser and better, and deadlier. And since I've always been thirsty to fight, if a fight were to pop off, as each opportunity presented itself would have been accomplished since I'm known to have a smart mouth, very petty, revengeful, equaling to what others say that I'm something else.

Again only God Himself only knows what will really happen in my life, and only he knows where I would be in life as of 2015, especially when too many people my age died before me and some messed up ways to sad, wrongfully, unexpected ways. I can tell you I wouldn't have the life I have now because God allowed me to become disabled in the process. It may have been a sad way, yet God knows what He's doing. He himself puts a blessing in the storm, and God works in funny, strange, marvelous, unexpected ways. Only he knows what and who he saved me from having STDs, being killed, raped, emotionally becoming a bomb if not living like one before I die, crackhead, suicidal, etc. I firmly believe/know God makes no mistakes, and I can preach all day long talking about him in this book, yet before I throw some words in my book about God and how I feel about him, let me first tell you how I feel about life.

Look at life and how life works from my eyes and not the eyes of those who are ungrateful about their family, from the ones who've been fed with a golden spoon to the people who understand having nothing to something only supporting yourself in a world that's about money, sex, technology, and drugs and what we all must do just to survive. I want others to know how it feels to be/ feel/ do things alone, feeling like the world is against you with their hands out. Before I can go further about this topic, you first have to understand my emotions, what I've been through, seen, dealt with, just to understand where I'm coming from. Before I preach about God and tell people how the world really is about from my eyes looking from the inside to the outside and how the world could have been if it was the way God wanted it and again, he knows how to keep the peace, joy, happiness which explain why there's such a thing called sin. So, I thank God for the life I have now (even though I don't understand it all just yet) and not for where it could have gone.

I'm convinced that both you and I know God saved me. I may not be aware of what I'm here for or why he saved me, yet I should find out in due time since His will for me shall be my WILL to complete. If I lived the fantasy life, I know I would be the sheep who left his/her shepherd and will never be found. God knows how to get a spirit's attention when needed, and he caught my undivided attention over the twenty-three years of my life I've lived so far, and like the pastor said, "If it wasn't for the Lord who was/is on my side where would be?" Again only God knows the real answer, especially living in this world, this generation, in this lifetime. I know for a fact that my hope and faith will be no more.

I'm not proud of the life I came from, yet I learned more in this life than what I would have learned in my fantasy lifestyle. My flesh wishes it lived to avoid the lifestyle I'm living now and would have sent my soul to hell. The life I live now is meant for me in today's world, lifestyle, society because of how today's lifestyle is now set up and how it (America) started from the time Columbus and his people took over the country for religious freedom and much more not caring that the land was already occupied by the indunas who was clearly there before Columbus arrived. Since then, through school to how I look at life, America went from the building stages to letting technology take over (not realizing what people are doing), followed by all the wars and hate toward one another to not allowing people to enter America as if that's not how North America started out. Although we all stay in America, there are many levels and backgrounds. You will never know a person based on their looks.

The point I'm about to make now is how I look at life versus how life seems to us, all versus how God would have loved things to be done in the next two topics I will talk about later in this book. *James 2:5 my beloved brother, have not God chosen the poor (me) of the world, rich in faith and heirs of the kingdom which he has promised to those who truly loves Him?* Or another way you can read it is: *Has not God chosen those who are poor in the eyes of the world to be rich in faith and in their positions as believers and to inherit the kingdom of God which he has promised to those who loves him.* Read the scripture, let it marinate in your mind, and think about what that scripture is telling you, just as I sat and reread it several times to fully understand what God's saying to us all.

How The World Made Me Look At Life

Things won't always go your way in this lifetime, and the world (United States) revolves around money and technology running against time. America is a country that goes by every man for themselves and is not a country but more like a business, and business only competing against the next person, finding a financial lane to stay in. Now legally, to survive in this world you need food, shelter, and clothes. To survive in this lifetime, you at least need food, which clearly costs those who don't grow their food to raise their own animals. We have to get it from the store for those who don't grow food or raise animals. To have shelter, you not only have to pay for a piece of land but also have to pay bills that are set up from trash to water to heat and much more from a phone bill to cable bill and the list gets longer, especially for the people who have to have it all.

Clothes, of course, cost, should tell you that the world clearly is about money. My question is, why is this world about money? Better yet, why did the world teach us how it's about money? For one, we own nothing for what we are/were and will forever be here before and after us without the help from us but from God. So why should we continue to live for the money (devil) if we all still have to do our own work in our own ways just to survive? If we all grow our own food down to making our own clothes, our jobs will be to make sure each household is being well taken care of. If everyone were to mind their own business and not on the next person, then there wouldn't be time to do anything else. We're just simply becoming lays (sloth) as a country. Shout out to the man who came up with the idea of money... not.

Being in the world, men had time to think and come up with a tragedy to pay someone to do their work for them, but the next question would be, what will the person who worked for the money he/she worked for? The first thing to do is repeat the cycle to the next person so they will have a tendency to work for money. Then others will invent things that will make the people who earned/spend the money they just worked for, from pointless knickknacks and objects to the pointless toys we make today. I have to give it to the person behind this project that it's a way to control the world and our emotions, but it's doing more damage than good. People are judged looked at depending on how much money they spend/earn at the time. Again, we're only talking about spending money on food, shelter, and clothing (the three things we need to consider living or serving). Why are there bills if we all are supposed to be in this world with the same agenda to live life? Why not let bills be free since we need water, heat, and lights? We're nothing but living off a large piece of land surrounded by water and islands.

Instead of the three classes high, middle poor, if we were to live as the bible demonstrates, from helping/giving to one another when needed, for God is well pleased with those who give from the heart for it's better to give than to receive. The other part in the bible was to love thy neighbor as yourself, so logically why not? Why not treat the next person as you would want to be treated yourself no matter who the next person was?

The two simple rules/commands God commanded, and now I know and understand why he commanded them two rules just to keep peace away from the chaos. We all are witnesses to all the chaos that goes on now and much more, depending on what level of life you are currently living. If we never sin from the start, the world wouldn't be as it is now. Clearly, God made rules/sin commands for a reason to keep peace and order since we, the people, don't know how to function correctly without having rules, limitations, and boundaries. For nothing we are and nothing, we shall become after all is said and over with.

What kills me is when someone thinks highly of themselves than the next person as if we're not made the same way, by the same person for the same reason. Again, this is only trying to survive in the world. We're only get judged by the money we have or don't have. Then there are the jobs being made to doctors to lawyers to strippers to your average drug dealer to the hairstylist to being a sales associate to making music to selling pussy, and much more that is all done in return for money just so we use it for the things we want and need, not caring about killing the animals for food, clothes, and ownership. Then we again get judged based on what we can afford to do with the money we earn.

For many, you'll never know what you would do for some money, especially if the price is right. That is some dangerous stuff in my eyes, and again this is how the world is set up to be, not how I feel nor look at it. Still, I will state my opinion on how I feel about the world before I end this topic. Think about if everything were how God intended to be, how much more peaceful the world could have been. Unfortunately for us, money is the rule of all evil, and technology will be the downfall since we, the people, are more focused on the future and relying on technology more heavily and putting our trust in something we've created that can/will be destroyed. Then it's the obsession we want, which clearly will cost us. So the question is, how are we going to continue to receive money to get what we think our hearts' desire?

Clearly, that's where the many jobs come in. You mean to tell me I was born in this world (which costs just to give birth), schooled on different ways/opportunity to earn money (if I was to pass the OGT test in the state of Ohio) to obtain a job, so you can survive in the world, further my education to get a chance at a better opportunity to make more money just to be able to spend it how you would like to spend it then wait to die (which cost just to bury a loved one). It costs to check your health and get assistance at a nursing home. It costs just to live there at the nursing home since no one that works there wouldn't want to help you without them getting paid since no one does anything out of love anymore. As always, as soon as the cycle starts and repeats itself, it's impossible to stop man-made. So since you get the picture that no matter what we do or who we are as a person, we will forever need money to survive. How should I then look at life after it's telling me I need money just to survive, and it costs just to teach a kid how to make money, yet it's not enough to make real, big money to be a comfortable middle class without the college experience?

The two main things about politics are divided into republican or democrat, which majority of the middle class and low-class roots for the democrat voters, which again is nothing but about money. Why not let money be a nonexistent problem for us all as a planet and not a country? Why not get treated equally, treating the next person as if you were treating yourself? If we did it that way, there would never be a problem from having babies, working, and dying knowing the cycle we are living in now knowing people are being born each day as well as people dying. We should be aware of our position/role in life do/complete your position regardless of your position. It's temporarily yours as long as you shall live to do that position until you die.

Now ask yourself this: name one thing that will/can/shall last in this lifetime besides God and his words? Think about the music, clothes, and food relationships to feelings. The answer to the previous question is that nothing will ever last in this lifetime besides God and his promises. For heaven and earth shall pass, but his word will stay and not be returned void. So if we can logically know and consume this, why not play the role (of your choice) just to survive and help the next to live a life since we are counting down as each second/minute passes us by for time is not yet on my side and never was in this lifetime since the first sin was committed.

We're all living in this lifetime just to live. Like Tupac said, "Why are we dying to live when we're just living to die?" Let's just say everyone did their job, and instead of doing it for money, they did it out of love. What if we could travel the world for free and vacation for free out of love to working at a store serving food of all kinds to personal items to clothing again, all free out of the spirit of love/showing/feeling loved? This includes bills to insurance to even gas (I believe we're using it wrongfully since we're polluting the world), and what comes up shall surely come down. Anyway, if everything we do/ did was out of love, how peaceful and equal the world would be. Especially if we were going by the rules/commands, we were told just to keep from chaos, for there's a thing as evil, and it can or will come in the strangest ways, and that's why life is the way it is now.

If people realized that this world and its lifetime is not about us or what we want/need but about God and how he used his only begotten son Jesus Christ as our Lord and personal savior just to shut it down at the end. Still, for those who know this, why not actually do what we're supposed to do and try to do the right thing as far as living a life that is not easy to live? If we know that, then we know how the next person feels as well as yourself about life. The way wealthy people live their lives from rappers, singers, and artists of all sorts have visions and dreams and trials and tribulations from time to time while others live a rough life and die the same way. Then there are the ones who make it out of the hood, yet we all as a country fail to realize and understand other people's backgrounds, ways, and emotions. We only tell you what we feel we should tell you, and that's it. Again, all we really think about is money, how to get it and what to spend it on. Of course, sex and drugs come in and play their role, but cash overrules it all, for both sex and drugs sell for those who make money off it.

Logically, we think and care about ourselves and how much it costs to live a lifestyle we dream to live. It's sad already that it costs to have a baby to bury a loved one, regardless of who you were or did. The holidays, concerts, and even water, which was here before our time, to the trash that's being shipped to other parts of the land as if we can continue this cycle forever all cost money. Holidays are made to make extra money and feel emotional. Water should never cost, and trash will build up, backfiring on the world for making trash and junk in the first place. For those who are atheists, ask yourself this: what will happen to the world after we've destroyed it? Better yet, who can fix this problem besides God Himself?

Everything from perms/relaxers to lotion and soap, it all costs, and we all need money to maintain items we use in our everyday lives. In our minds, it's been about, taught to us, and will forever be about money and getting as much of it as possible (greed and glutting, which are two more of the seven deadly sins) just to solve most of life's problems, especially for all those go-getters and strugglers to the hustlers. Whether good or bad, we all have the same mindset to get enough money, legally or illegally. Money will get you what you want, how you want it, when you want it done, depending on how much money you want to get and who you are/know. Plus, people always go by the reputation you bring with the money. Then again, money qualifies who you are as a person and what people see you as (being on the outside looking in), not individual, whether you think who you are is really who you are as a person, or you were pretending to be. Yet actions and words do all the walking and talking for you.

Now that you have a clear vision of how life is/was taught to us, I need money to do anything, stay anywhere, determine how I should look at life, and what should be my motto? To get money, forget these niggas and live the life you want/need. No matter who you are from, rich or poor, your motto is to get money since that's what the schools taught us. This was what life was really about. So in my mind, it is set to get money any way I can get it. Find your sport/position in life and do what you have to do to get what you need to get to do what your heart desires but mainly needs. Meaning I'm going to do anything necessary just to make a decent lifestyle. There's not even a need for me to have a funeral for people (if any were to show) to cry at the sight of my body since my spirit is no longer there, so forget my body/appearance. Nor do I feel like I would be remembered for who I was by the time I am scheduled to die, so it will be pointless to have/pay for a funnel or to even get married since that to cost along with being divorced.

This lifetime is again about money and getting it anyway/spending it anyway anyhow. So people expect you to get the big picture about life as we see it and do their individual parts whether they have to have an opportunity to live a regular life every person wishes they had. However, the story goes, we all have the same agenda. So, those who have a clear picture of how I feel, who I am, and what I want/need money for just to live, and no, it's not fair. Even though I have a check in the system and am disabled, I'm far from satisfied. For one, the none sewing part of the doctor's mistakes or whatever happened since I wasn't born into the world disabled. For two, a check and food stamps shouldn't satisfy me or the next person receiving handouts.

Like Joule said, "*Mama, dry your eves, there's no reason to cry, you made a genius and I isn't gone take it for granted, I isn't gone settle for less, I isn't gone take what they hand me, I'm a take what they owe me and show you that I can fly and show old dude what he's missing, the ills*

nigga alive, now who am I." That whole statement should

apply to everyone, especially blacks knowing what our

ancestors went through.

Back to the topic, no one should ever be satisfied

receiving handouts, being on a budget to live a life you can

afford. Why? If I were to have my check and was allowed

to spend it on anything besides what I needed to spend it

on, that still would limit how much money I was allowed to

spend that month. Any person's dream is to never receive

anything they love or desire limited, no matter what it is

from sex, weed, money, etc. Also, I strongly dislike the

poor class lifestyle. You and everyone else deserve to have

or do things you once planned to do far as being successful

in something that's leading you to live a comfortable

lifestyle you shouldn't be able to complain about.

For I too desire to do things that I've planned my

entire life, and each day goes by with me, you, others doing

whatever, whether it's working on your dreams to giving up

on your dreams, the day is getting closer to your appointment with death that you cannot miss out on or reschedule. So how/why should I continue living the way I am now as I write this book, still feeling how I feel and stay like this until my last breath? I feel my existence in life is greater than settling for a check and dying. Do you think I won't feel any type of way? That's only living-wise and not emotional-wise.

I realize I'm not satisfied with a check, so I seek other ways to earn income to have a well affordable lifestyle that I won't complain about it. Not telling you how I would be getting my extra income to get a lifestyle of my choice, just know with the same spirit/mindset, I would have the same plan as everyone else, which is to get money. I will do damn near anything to get/obtain a lifestyle to avoid sleeping outside in the cold, rain, snow, weather, who knows where surrounded by evil people, their ways and thoughts and action and think I can get a good night's sleep. Heck no. To avoid becoming a bum being homeless, no matter how your story is/went down the drain, I can't/refuse to since my emotions wouldn't take it without committing suicide from depression and no value since I need money just to qualify me as a person.

We all play this game of life just how the world is showing us to be, feel, and endure it all, regardless of our lifestyle and situations. I could have been like everyone else, caring and worrying about myself and doing what I have to do to get to where I'm going. No matter what I had to do or whom I had to cross, I'll be thinking and focusing on myself and what I need, which is nothing but money. The sad part about it is that it's not about the money but about the things we want to do that you need the money to do it for. Money is just a piece of paper that controls what life we're allowed/can live, emotion, loyalty, respect, and self-worth and again qualifies who you are as a person.

If there was no money in the world, what would be the next best thing in the world we'd use to get things done around here? Since it is a thing as money and me being the person I am, the question would be, what will I do for some paper? Maybe the question should be, what wouldn't I do for some paper? Knowing the life I lived, being exposed to, and where I came from (Cleveland, Ohio) and we all know where I'm trying to go in life. No matter what I had to do to get it, I would have gotten it. For we all bought the same dream. We just chased different routes and paths. Being in love with themselves is something the bible talks about, and by the fantasy life I would have loved to live, but that saying in the bible would have implied to me.

That's the best way to demonstrate how I would have lived my life if it weren't for my disability. Since I have a check, plus looking for more ways to make more money, I'm searching for why God kept me here this long. Yet I might have a clue or just faith that God will slowly guide me to where I'm supposed to be, for He hears my cries and screams that I've cried and screamed since I was a kid. The way the world is set up now is no help on how an individual feels inside. Being in this world tells a person what to do, not to do to avoid future problems if possible. If I was broke, nowhere to go, nothing to eat, nothing to wear up would have become careless to the world. If I continued to stay in my low class and accept whatever they handed me my way, followed by the competing others to prove I'm better than the next, complaining about what I want and don't have, acting how your average broke person will act. That's also always minding someone's business but their own but desire to seek attention, entertainment, settle for less, including a house and food. Yet they still manage to complain about what they want, have sex, use the little money given to them, and afford what they can get, wish for a change, but do nothing to change. They slowly become insane, repeating the cycle with their offspring. Some just love others, not realizing it costs to even love someone from marriage to having a baby to losing a loved one. You need money just to survive and have it all.

Other poor people hustle and plan not to stay that way for long. Their ambition is to be what drives them to find a better opportunity to gain money and chase their dreams. The majority watch life goes by with wishes, hopes, dreams, regrets, drama, drugs, sex, and sloth.

However, the middle class has a job whether they love their job or the pay and treat themselves to a decent lifestyle that they can afford. It may not be what they like/want, but they can't complain, for it could be/get worse than what it already is. They have fewer wants and needs thanks to the income they receive to solve most of their problems. They have a better opportunity to make and maintain money and do as they wish or can afford to do. Again, they might not have it all but a suitable life they can afford from a nice house to a nice car and afford to help other family members in need.

The difference between the poor and middle classes is that most of the middle class work their butts off to get what they want, whether it was easy for them to do it or not, or about where they came from, whether from fortunate or unfortunate ways. While most of the poor do nothing but complain about the difference, both parties are eager to get money. Then the high class uses the money to make more money, whether they invest in a company or their offspring's education. However they choose to do it, they do it so they can afford to spend it on what they want/need/ desire. They will invest because they fear losing money and becoming poor, so they make sure they find a way to make more money while still spending money. They have a great opportunity to become what/who they want to become with the power of money and who you know. Kids have better school systems to attend, yet the schools want money to teach kids to make good money. They have fewer problems and desires of what they want and need since they can solve most problems from bills to keeping gas in the car. They can afford to take care of another family, whether for a short time period or until death.

It's simply about your money and how much you have/maintain. Most of the high class can get whatever their heart desires depending on who they know and what they want done. Then those wealthy families who actually use the money to solve any problems they may come across with. They live life grateful. Some are ungrateful since they can't imagine how it is to be without, to live carefree, or worry less about anything. They have families and can afford a lifestyle of any choice. They couldn't care less if the next person were struggling to let all ends meet to others feeling abandoned and neglected while others feel bad for the unfortunate. They just live life the best way they can and wait to die since we all have to die. Some may pay attention/love things more than people developing a relationship with that thing, and by having that thing/item, lust, feelings that will not last yet, love can last and is a gift you can confuse to receive and give out.

The common thread to all five classes (bomb, poor, middle, high, wealthy) is no matter who you are or what you do to what you desire, if you want a place to call home to eat as well as pay bills, you need money regardless of who you are as a person. Again, the only race that my heart goes out to be the blacks. How should blacks feel getting told that our value was worthless and act upon it by the constant rejection of not getting justice, me being one of the many? So, if we're left with no hope/help, what shall then go through our minds? Better yet, how should we react to it? Shoot, blacks only used gangs on the west coast for respect and power like the white men and control in order in a community filled with hopeless, doubtless people designed not to make it from the bottom. Blacks went from slavery to establishing a struggling, less ornate lifestyle and were only accepted in certain areas to live to deal with rejection from jobs, houses, schools as if that's not going to make us mad, let alone the next person.

Because we went through job hiring/losses, causing the black families to live a tough life, having their offspring experience a more challenging lifestyle becoming more hopeless and heartless. I mean, ask yourself, how would you feel going through all that blacks went through, or how would you feel watching a loved one go through what blacks go through? It's the fact that blacks are the only race who came to America with nothing. We had to forcefully work for free, were slaves, then freed with nothing offered to them other than segregation and wrongful justice because of the color of our skin. Salute to those who make it out of the hood/ghetto to have a comfortable, affordable life. Shootout to the ones trying to make it in life. I feel sorry for those who gave up or cared about belittling themselves or the people around and after them.

See, the purpose of the pain and the suffering is to witness it up close and personal on how it feels to be without can relate to others and their pain, trials, and tribulations, and only through the pain shall we grow from it. I see daily other people still living off their past failures to make a change yet only repeating the same pattern and the next generation becoming like their parents, not breaking the cycle. We all have different habits and ways we got from birth parents just like how we have God's ways, likes, tastes, sense of humor to gifts giving a piece of him to us all just as we have a piece of our parents with us, through us, and within us. I, for one, got the hustling, making money by any means necessary from my mom to cleaning and not like repeating myself from going crazy and much more all from my dad. I got using people, what's benefiting me if I do a task for someone's, to smoking weed to partying and turning up to my tongue out and more from my dad.

The difference between my parents and me is that I use all personalities and traits from both and use them defiantly in my own unique way just to live in today's world, which is a game about money. Most friendships, others are for the money/what you can do for that person who is about to use you if you want to confuse the fake friendship people have among others for whatever reason they have to befriend you whether a friendship to a spouse. Another difference between couples and single people is most couples are supposed to work as a team to get/spend money to live a life. Singles do it by themselves (for those who don't have a family to help, look out for, support to motivate people). However, in 2015 in today's world, it's all over the place, and I've had a front seat to seeing couples taking advantage of others and using each other. Or maybe one is using one while the other is being used, allowing them to be used, and does nothing about it but complain about it.

Some just worry about themselves and are inconsiderate of others. Yet all parties have the same agenda: "we need money" no matter what lifestyle you came from/want to relationship status. Without it, you might as well become the ground, be walked on, or like the wind and invisible to the world. Is it sad to teach the world that life is about money when it's supposed to be about love? Whether money or off the stretch of love, things will still have to get/be done whether we were to do the work with others or by ourselves just to survive in this world. Logically once a human/living thing they're alive and exist in an unknown place, its habit agenda is to do anything and everything to maintain what you have now consumed/felt/experienced and try to remain satisfied for the time being here on earth. It focused on maintaining satisfaction since we're in an unknown place, by an unknown person (yet) confused how we even got here.

Of course, we want answers, which can lead to confusion in which people can be misled from earthly things to manmade things. Yet, we have all agreed to use the money to survive, not understanding nor realizing with money or not, we will still have to survive as well as we're destroying our planet cutting our oxygen supply day by day. So, if you know that, why not the world as a whole again, make it easy for one another to live a life and survive and not to live hard but at least since we as a plant disagree on the reason living here on earth. This, in my opinion, is to love one another, and again everything we need to survive and need was already here provided to us through the help of God. Thanks to him, we need nothing else. So again, why make the world difficult when it doesn't have to be as we make it in today's world.

It's very simple and common sense that we all want to live a simple life, and when I mean simple, I mean the actual definition of a smile. The sad part about it is that we use most animals for food, clothes, etc. The ones we lock in a cage at a zoo (their version of shelter) know us as a whole (all living things) have the same agenda as the next, which is to survive. The difference between us and other living things is that they don't pay bills, have a job, money, or house, but we all manage to live and "survive" in this world. So again, no matter what we do or who we are as humans, we need money to survive and live in this world, which is the point I'm making. Plus, the simple fact that this world taught us that, so the question is, how should we interpret that in our minds? Get this money with or without the next person. How should we look at life? How should a person feel for themselves, let alone another person just the way my generation was taught, those who led the ones who taught us, us who's teaching the next generation, and the cycle begins to look out for yourself and your loved ones.

Revenge, when needed, doesn't care for the next as if that's a cool, free, peaceful, happy way to live. I just wish people would open their eyes to what we're facing, about to face, and have faced. I'm not just talking about death, but the creator who created us for clearly common sense let us know we didn't create ourselves for we will be able to continue to do that, nor do we have every answer to every question we've asked or will ask in the future. Do know and understand where I'm coming from, referring to while others hear me, but they don't feel me, and the rest may let it go in one ear and out the other, not paying attention to one thing I have to say/feel the need to say. We fail to realize or care about the world revolving around money and technology, slowly destroying our minds. Our minds are something that we do not know all its capability of, understand, or realize just yet.

Then sex is selling and pleasing our flesh. I'm one of the many to admit I use sex in more than one wrongful/unpleasant way, along with drugs and other stuff that will/can/shall destroy our bodies if we were allowed to live long enough to watch ourselves self-destruct from liquor to fatty food to tobacco. We all do it, knowing its consequences, but most importantly, what do we need to complete these desires/lustful things? Money. There are so many rules minus the free sex for those who just have sex to feel it. Money makes the dream/fantasy/order, self-respect, self-esteem, and the list can go longer from vacations and traveling to taking care of the sick to those in need. Clearly, we already know that we eat, sleep, shit, but also, we walk on money, stare at money (painting), wear money, the act of learning something new that costs as well but for the first person who knew what we now know was free to her/him/them.

Again, to make something shake, we simply use money to learn things, whether we were to base it on examples, facts, or tests. If we didn't don't do the same research that the original person told us, how would we know what was told/taught to us was even true? However, we use money to confirm the information that we were told is true, trusting the person by bribing them with cash just to do the work for you. So again, the question for you is, what wouldn't you do for some money?

My question is what I wouldn't do for some money after being exposed to what I've been exposed to, witnessed, experienced, and felt inside a world full of other people and their lives. Some people's lives are similar, while others have no clue of the "hard life" and what others have to do to try to get somewhere in life just to survive. Then the majority fantasy about how their life could have been just like my fantasy about my life. Since I'm now an adult and have known/witnessed the world differently from what I was first taught, minus God and what we are as a country, makes the world seem different. How shall I now look at life plus adding what I feel already been exposed to versus what I already learned, what I witnessed, versus what I was told versus how I feel. So, having a clue on how my mind is, thinks, and feels, how then shall I live my life, let alone feel about it? However, before I answer that, let me tell you how I look at life before telling you how I feel.

My Version Of Life In "The Streets"

Taking a step down the path that I've experienced/gone through first assumed this was everyone's life, just different people. I expected everyone to have the same mother that I had and live the same lifestyle I lived, but as I got older, I saw otherwise. It isn't as bad as what people make it seem like depending on what area of the projects. Some are familiar with the lifestyle of living in the projects, while others may have a clue based on movies of how it is to live and be in the projects. In my case, staying on the east side of Cleveland, Ohio, you have different projects from 30th (dirty 30s) to the Garden Valley on East 79th in Kinsman to 55th in Case, where I stayed for a couple of years until I moved to Broadway, which is still down the street from 55th projects.

Depending on the area of the projects, you have roaches bed bugs, and only God knows what else is down there. However, I can proudly/boldly say my mom never had the roach problem staying in the CMHA, and she was/is a clean freak, something both my parents are. Then there are those until this day that I sit and watch/witness them have a severe roach problem. When I say too many, I mean they were plentiful, from coming out of beds and mattresses to sockets outlet at one house to roaches coming out the toilet to the stoves and fridge at another home. I strongly dislike roaches and any other insects for my own personal reasons, but that wasn't the only places roaches were at. Just the projects will be the most common place to find roaches and other critters.

That was one of my big peeve/nightmares to even see one, which I slowly overcame over the years thanks to visiting/staying over other people's houses from the projects to MLK Street off Kinsman to the people in the Valley. Anyway, I watched my mom work, mourning her mother's death and much more. She went through a failed relationship leading to a divorce for the first time (something I consider to never happen), leading her to raise four kids on her own with food stamps (I was unaware until the age of seventeen) and an SSI check since I'm disabled. Still, only God knows the truth about that situation whether she had my check and not spending it on me or not to us relocating on Kinsman, the uptown area away from 93rd and below (which I dislike the areas from 93rd and below on both the east and west side of Cleveland).

Anyway, with the b.s. I went through with my mom and her bad habits and teaching us to get this money. I became being about money, making money, wanting to spend money for things like trips, clothes, vacations, site seeing, and much more. I loved going to the malls, especially Randall Mall, and shopping at my favorite stores, J.C. Penney and Footlocker. When it was open, on the east side of Cleveland on Miles, I was too thirsty to wear some new shoes with a new outfit. My mom did spoil us as little children before everything changed, and we barely wore an outfit a second time. That's how good my mom started off. She knew she needed money to do all those things, and she made sure she had it with no help from no one.

When my granny died, my mom and her entire family, from her kids to her siblings, died with her on February 7, 2000. When I say no help from no one, I mean no one on both my mom's mother to my mom's father's side of the family. My granny's only help from family members on both sides was when she first got sick. Some helped clean, some helped cook maybe three times, then there was no more, and my mom was left with her four kids. No one really cared for us, besides three to five cousins who cared but wanted/couldn't be there for her or her four kids. If there was love in our family, it was never shown besides the most obvious fake love. People started showing (me realizing) after my granny died. So, I watched my mom and her four grow up isolated from our family, minus the cousins we saw once in a while, plus the few who stay on the same street as my mom. Unfortunately, the ones who stayed on my mom's street are now dead minus three people, and the last one got killed on July 31st (Long live

Murddy). Other than those few people, we lived and experienced life isolated/alone by the age of ten.

Through all of what my mom was going through, I was unaware of at first, she made sure she didn't go without. I mean, she had enough stuff that would last her months if something were to happen from clothes, food, household items, including the times we had to stay at hotels for she knows the reason she had to do that to always keeping a car no matter on how many cars she had to go through. She demonstrated how to become an independent woman and what it is/means to get a job done you need done just to survive since, again, we need money to survive and make a living. Mentally, I took that as a sign to always try to have my own and never go without. Because she stacks up on stuff, I now do the same as I write this book. She told me to make some money whether or not I had to sell something.

Again it takes money to make money, and she didn't have to tell me that, but she showed it, and I watched her and took notes. The best part about my life was although I went through some mental and physical things, we could never say my mom's house went without, and I was grateful in a few ways. I knew/heard of people and families that get raped, from having to eat cold hotdogs, sugar water, or bread, having no clothes, or visiting the Goodwill/thrift for hand-me-down clothes. Through all I went through with my mom, I couldn't imagine her being like this, let alone her kids, even though I felt simulates with others since my older brother and I could barely eat to having scraps to the way I was treated to the way my mom beat me with many different objects. Those who read my first book know exactly what I'm talking about. Then I see the ones who had clothes to parents who showed them love, attention, affection to them receiving money, just to spend it on who knows what, to parents letting them do as they please. Having a definition of a cool parent while I had no freedom and went straight home most days until the day my brother left me, and I was about to be sixteen.

After my granny died, her other two siblings died after, and soon after, their father died. My mom then got sick and was diagnosed with Lupus. She slowly stopped working, yet she tolerated everything. She went from working at Tower City in Downtown Cleveland banking to retiring from the workforce, opening a mini store out of her house, and boy, we went the hell and back twice, selling every and anything she bought and sold back. We even went to flea markets to sell her stuff, and my mom was the one telling us what to do while my older brother and I sold the merchandise, getting no money for the hours working for her. My mom was simply money-hungry like her two oldest children are. When I say she was selling everything, I mean clothes, shoes, cleaning products, and other household items, fragment smells, on top of food to beer to cigarettes. The only thing she didn't sell was hard liquor.

Mom made tons of cash selling out her home and had my brother and I sell some stuff in middle school during lunchtime, even to the dinners our school ordered. Since my mom stayed less than three minutes from our school, she was the delivery girl. This was another idea in my head, for again, she showed me that it takes money to make money, and I'm very confident that the people reading this book agree with me as well. She took no days off, having my brother and I sell her merchandise while she got paid for it. We went from flea markets to the Bureau County Fair to our family church to other churches selling everything she bought or stole. I mean, she had toilet brushes to thermal socks to movies to mini back massages and more. She supported her and her two youngest children while her oldest two dealt with the many customers. Still, she managed to stack up on everything she put her hands on.

I had never seen my mom without anything from tissue to cleaning products. She would run to the store to reload if she were getting low on the items she needed since she never wanted to run out of anything. From clothes to food to household items, including the times we traveled to Florida to Canada, she always brought too much of everything, even switching up on cars each time we visited where our great grandma is from.

The only bad part about my childhood was the constant mental and physical abuse she showed her kids, mainly my brother and me. My mother did more damage to my mind and soul than all the physical beatings she did on my body with the many objects she managed to get her hands on. Sadly, this included bending my fingers on both hands to digging into my skin every time she was to squeeze my neck. At least my mom wasn't like the other parents living in the street, off the government, with their hands out receiving food stamps, welfare checks, and free insurance. Then again, the hell if I know what all she'd done, but regardless, my mom wasn't the type of woman who sits on her ass and do nothing with her life but wish for a change without attempting to make that wish/dream come true like I see parents to my generation are doing now as I write this book. They do it to get a certain amount of money to afford a low-income housing project/ living arrangement in an area that is full, surrounded by the same people, similar stories, and different backgrounds. Some have jobs. Others are jobless. People who aren't for families, especially for the many children who have been in the foster care system, whether you were taken from your parents to your parents putting you in there, giving up on their blessings God blessed the parents with.

Then there's that Cleveland school system under the Ohio law that isn't as good as the other schools in Cleveland that are private or charter schools and cost extra to get a better education that will be used for money. Those schools have a better chance of being looked/reviewed on a transcript when attending a college just so the person can have a better chance at making a lifestyle of their choice (food, shelter, clothes). All schools have an opening to have one of their students get drafted to a college where money will give you the education to consider yourself to apply for a job. Many like you will apply since we all have the same dream we were taught to have, which was to live a life you can comfortably afford to live with or without the next person. The goal is to have it all, never to go or be without, for again, money tells us the level of humanity we're actually in, whether we're poor. People care less about the less fortunate or wealthy, and everyone knows of you and wants to hear your opinion about things.

All schools in Ohio have to pass the OGT first before allowing other students to walk the stage and enter the beginning of adulthood. Both my parents and teachers never prepared me for the next stage of my life. They may have scholarships available for those in sports or winning an essay contest, and much more, yet private and charter get the first dibs on that before the public school system does. If you discover your talent at an early age, you may or may not get a scholarship to help pay for your first four years of college based on your talents. Those who don't have an equal opportunity to attend college find other ways to make it to college using financial aid (me) while the majority (me) fall off the college train due to financial problems, while some stay longer than others.

Again, high school never really prepared us for the next few steps/routes we have to take to get where we're trying to go as a generation. Parents who can't afford the private school system (my mom put my younger siblings through the system until middle/high school) are left with the public system and might have a chance to further their education to qualify to go off to college. Then some can't even make it to college for multiple reasons, from financial problems to not passing the test. Some just settle for a job if they can find employment, while others live for love/searching for it in all the wrong places, getting left with a broken heart/dreams with kids, stuck following their parents/ others' footsteps. All parties will receive anything given to them by the system for the little help the government gives the citizens of America. Some turn it into more money from selling their food stamps to make more money to sell what they can afford to sell, while others do nothing but settle for whatever is given to them and make it work the best way they know how.

Too many street people live "the settling for less" lifestyle of getting told monthly how much money to receive just to do whatever we please. Or we live whatever lifestyle we can afford to live with the money and keep it pushing, making the little money we receive work. This one refuses to live/stay like this in this lifestyle, but before I say more, first picture yourself again being me, living my life the way I've lived it in the past, how my mind is set up from being physically/mentally/emotionally hurt? How would you mentally handle and look at life? If not being raised, seeing people struggle badly, settle for less, and watch life pass you by. I watched others make money and do as they please as we all wish we were free to do, all as if I could jig and be comfortable with living how I see others as if I would be in any better situation than the next if we all are doing nothing but sit on our behinds, being told what to do and how, or when to do it.

After that, the only other thing is to make something shake to get some money only because I care how my mom handles her life, not what she did or how she did it, but the fact that she did it. Due to the many boundaries she set for me, not to mention having the motto to want and desire to have and keep because of the feeling of spending it on getting what your heart wants/desire.

The school just confirmed my mom's motto *to get money to survive*. No matter what it is, I need money to do it and only money. So if the world told me that's what it's about, I was planning on getting it and giving it to the world in exchange for the freedom/lifestyle of my choice. It told me to do what I had to do for life itself makes it be about money, so get with the program or stay in the poor class system. We as a country designed a successful project to hinder blacks and those who don't have what it takes, no matter what it is, to make money and let others who are struggling to make ends meet. They were set to stay in the poor class system since the poor class (those who are trying to better themselves and their situation) only have just enough to make it but not enough to make it out of the poor system.

Again, this is what the government helped set up and is successful in today's life as I write this book. However, everyone has a personal story, but mine was that I had nothing nor was anything given to me but food stamps and an SSI check. I wasn't fed with a golden spoon, so if I want/need something, I'd better become like my mother and go out there and get it by any means necessary if I had to. So mentally, as I witnessed around me, we as Ohio, let alone a country, have to maintain life by maintaining shelter, food, clothing, cleaning products, and much more. Every person is now responsible for their responsibilities/hidden skills to survive, and again the money tells what financial level you're on.

In my case, staying with my mom, I realized no one was there to help, save, rescue, save me from my nightmare of reality, but a check came unexpectedly, and I took that and ran without looking back. Like 2Chainz, the rapper, *"My momma said fuck it nigga. Hit the streets and live. Found a check in the system, and I did what I did."* Real talk, I discovered the check when I was eighteen, yet the offer never justified whatever happened to me as an infant. In my eyes, that monthly check is not enough to justify whatever happened to me, my hand, my foot, and my brain/emotions. So, how should I feel about receiving a certain amount monthly to live a life I can afford with the check? So how can you set a limit on my life and how much I can get/spend on living since, again, the world is taught about getting/making money? How am I supposed to feel about this life as a person, let alone a woman? That's again only to survive minus the things I want/desire to have/want/wish or to do in my life as I get closer to my death date since time again is not on our side. I walk around and see, sense, and feel people are out for themselves or simply against families/friends.

As I grew up, the completion of who's better than the next has been around before my time. With money, they can solve the question we think we have to the logic "who's better than the next", not realizing that nothing we once were and nothing we can/shall be, for without God we're nothing; just like a soul with no body to a heart with no beat to it. So why should I have to consider myself financially stable/defying a lifestyle that I want to live when all the material things from Gucci, Louie, Prada to Versace has nothing to do with life or what life's about, nor does it have anything to offer as far as what's already in the world before our time? And not what we have to use that's already here to make something that may seem better until the cycle repeats itself and we seek to find the new temporarily best thing that's not going to last as long as we wish for it to last. Today's world, especially in this and the generation after us, is always and forever looking for the new best thing, which is the technology that money makes happen. Again, thanks to the world itself, it's telling me to get money and if you want to live and not become a homeless bum, unimportant, asking for handouts, or accepting for less.

It feels better to give than to receive, and I agree with him, for he finds pleasure in that, and it's the feeling you get when you help the next person making their day seem better than what it already is. Still, as we use it in today's world, these food stamps and welfare "handouts" are nothing but modern-day slavery. They tell us again what lifestyle we're qualified to live as if everyone wants to sit on their butts and live off a budget like receiving food stamps, welfare, SSI check was enough when we were taught in school that there is no limit. It was the sky if it was a limit, but it is far from food stamps/welfare checks.

Now I must be honest. The feeling of giving to one another to receive something from someone is good, but in my case, receiving food assistance to my SSI is not a humble/pleasing/grateful feeling but more of an unappreciative of it. The level of where you must go/trying to go in life to receive the handouts hurts you, your mind, and your emotions. Some are immune to it, taking whatever is given becoming a leech. Instead, we live life the best way we know how, comfortably, which came before our time. Whoever made/thought about money intended for their invention of making/creating money to control our lifestyle, emotions, loyalty toward one another, and much more. It does something to your mind, messing with your feelings and emotions based on money and how much money we had just to live a life, something we were created to do, yet how we live as a country is clearly let alone the entire planet. So instead of loving like we were created to do, we live for the love of money.

For my side of town, you don't have to fend for and make your future better than your past. Whether you were to get the money legally or illegally, the motto is still the same: *to strive to the top of the pyramid and mountain money and consume it all.* You don't want to feel or experience how it is to be without it. To live life as carefree as we all want it to be and become worry-free, you need money to solve those emotional feelings, and if not, then watch it on the sidelines. Just as there are streets, there are also sidewalks for those who can't or won't fit in them.

When you're alone, and there's no one or nowhere to go, you automatically belong to the streets, which are nothing but a piece of land used for a bigger cause. The streets are unfair to be surrounded by and have no rules yet boundaries from don't snitch, don't get caught, do what you need/have to do to survive. It's not as bad as what people make it seem like depending on who you know, who you hang out with, or what you live in, fiending for someone or something to love, running into the streets with both open arms, hoping to love and trust someone or something again. Usually, they are the same ones running from something or someone looking for someone to befriend, feel important to someone, or fix what's broken. They don't realize those they are running to in the streets are also running, trying to get away from their past since they know how it feels to get/be hurt/betrayed.

You then substitute what you were running from to what you will have to run from in the future (those who make it out the street life) and become satisfied living in this country since we all technically are on the same level, just different paths, routes, direction, agendas yet the same mentally (majority). Since I have no family, no one to love, give/get affection, or be important to, I did what others did. From my cousin to my uncle to my brother, I chilled, kicked it, and befriended those who considered themselves part of the streets to avoid feeling alone/ my reality to use them as my entertainment memories to keep within myself, whether good or bad.

No matter what category you're under, we all have/had realized that we have to survive regardless of what we have to do to survive. Some in the street may understand the pain I/each other go through since pain led us all to the streets and deal with one another to not feel be/ alone. Others get the chance to achieve their personal dreams, whether it was a hard, painful way to achieve them, while the rest remained in the street. They may feel that no one truly cares for them, so why should they care for the next one or give them a chance to consider caring about the next as if we all aren't in the same situations being in the streets. We may come from a different background, yet you are on the same level, same situation, and same problems in the streets. However, as you enter the life of living in the streets, you learn several lessons that are better shown/demonstrated to you than someone overbearing telling you. The schools, including college life, can't even teach you the lessons you will learn. You're better at watching what's going on around you and in your circle of street friends you think you have and like a simple math problem. If things don't add up right, you need to subtract yourself from the situation. Problem solved. Then some live off their ambition, something my mom put in me. You will watch as others come from having nothing, then there's the one who had stuff from family to supporters to sponsors, but things changed.

No matter how you got out there in the streets alone, abated, finding for yourself. When you first enter the street, you will feel all the love of others who have nothing to gain or lose. Everything seems cool as your frowns turn upside down, yet the same people who make you laugh can/ shall make you cry again. Still, for a different reason, your past frowns as the acting stages are over and the people in the streets reveal how they really feel about you along with the next person, how you live your life, your wants/needs. They're about one person and one person only... themselves. In the beginning, you seem ok, and everything seems fine, and you begin to manage a lifestyle since everyone is trying to afford a comfortable lifestyle having everything they need. Still, you're unaware of how others truly feel about you now that you are considered to be just like them living on the same level being in the streets, what they're capable of doing, and how they can honestly care less about you, let alone one another. After all, no one cared for them, so why should they care about you and vice versa? Why should you expect loyalty, honesty, and trust from one another when the person who you first originally wanted it from couldn't give it to you?

The same way the next person living in the streets wanted the same thing you wanted from whoever hurt them, they grew to love, and something happened to us all that everything changed. From trusting one another to loyalty toward one another to being faithful and honest to one another, no matter what it was or who it was nor how it happened, when it happened, it changed you to something else that you can't turn back from. This includes old habits and now has a problem opening up to new people that they know nothing about nor care to know but what was told to them, if they choose to believe what was told to them is true or not.

So, when you first step out into the streets, you first believe everything and anything, trusting everything you see, hear, experience, and witness. You realize all you'll do is kick it with the different people in many ways. You know how to turn up with the different groups and crowds and go from a simple card game to gambling, drinking, smoking blazing music, and talking recklessly as the new sense of humor game, all hoping and wishing for the same get money game. Some handle business as far as living, making money again to afford a suitable lifestyle, while others take what they were given and keep it pushing while the rest do nothing but complain for a change. Then there are the ones whom we call "fuck boys" since they are only out to use you which every way, they can use you however they can use you and get what they can get and couldn't care less if you were to die the next day and won't shed a tear nor show up to your funeral. Then there are the ones I strongly dislike, and they're the ones who have nothing nor is trying to do anything but live off the next person becoming a leech and keep it pushing as if that's their new way of hustling/pimping someone into getting what you want as if that's cute or something.

There are also the "stick up" people who are simply heartless thieves who steal for personal reasons or purposes. They don't care who they're about to rob or their feelings from being robbed. They will show no remorse or mercy. Whatever they can get their hands on, they're taking it with no second thought about it. I respect all the real hustlers, from selling food, clothes, movies, weed/drops to body oil/ fragrance, and selling pushy to doing hair. Again, they use what they have/can do and turn it into money to live a life we all have to pay for, and since numbers don't even nor will the price of living have an extent, nine times out of ten they are the one that's in the category of street people who are different in their own unique way. However, all calories are left out here in the streets, isolated from the world, yet with the same agenda as the entire earth, which is to live, and in this lifetime to live, we need money.

Now there are homeless bums who also have personal gifts and talents who just have to start from the bottom of the life pyramid grid and struggle to get to the top if you want to live and if you can survive and maintain the struggle, then you shall make it for only the strong will win. No matter who you are or where you came from, once you're considered/qualified in the streets, you're in it, yet things from the streets seem/differ from the life you were born into. The love, tenderness, and grace toward one another are not shown in the streets, which is the beginning of your life changing for you.

People will steal from you for their own personal reasons, whether it's your peace, joy, or manmade items. They will speak falsely of you becoming jealous/envious in different ways, which turns into envy, and you are now the topic of the conversations to others. Secretly no one wants you to be/feel better than the next. For whatever reason, they feel the need to feel like that. Again you came into the streets/world trusting/ believing in everything you saw and was told, and when you enter the street, you start off partying, being friendly to all, yet people will show you how cruel they can get for whatever reason they had to be cruel for. When the act of a cruel person is shown to you, it changes you just as it changes the person who is being cruel to you, for no one was bone evil. However, we humans consume it with the flesh first to the spirit.

Again, some good-hearted people just happened to be in the streets surrounded by a world full of hopeless, ungrateful, hurtful people consuming everything they were exposed to and trying to channel it all, whether positively or negatively. Once you're in the streets and isolated from the world, you feel unimportant, unnoticed, unloved, and no one shows you any pity. People that have already been hurt will hurt you in various ways, not thinking or caring about how you feel, nor will they understand your feelings. Some will only use /be bothered with you if it benefits them, not you. Then you have those who only want you around to keep them from boredom. Watch out for all of them. Anyone and everyone are liable to kill you if you were to push them to the limit, for no one can honestly say they'll never kill a person until that opportunity presents itself. Decision-making can guide your actions into something or someone you never thought you could be or become in its rawest form. Just like you can never know what you don't need until you actually need it.

Anyway, again, there are no rules in the street game. Just mind your business, don't snitch, don't/can't trust cops, and trust no one. If you go by the rules alone, things are more bearable/manageable. Yet, because you're in this world living in this lifetime, no matter what you do for a living, who you are as a person, you will always have trials and tribulations period in your life. Everyone's life goal/agenda in the street is to make it where you're noticed, respected, and feared, regardless of your lifestyle in the streets. Since the world again is taught to be made about money just so we can live an affordable life, for those who aren't lazy to get out there and get the money themselves, we're going to get out there whether we have to do it legally or illegally. In the streets, people always scheme in making money. I know people who will purposely sell you some garbage weed to people giving their connect contraband just to sell what was given to them for free, all to just make some form of income. I honestly give them their respect for the hustle, but I don't respect the lack of love they show to one another. I know people who will steal movies just to sell them to people who strip, from my cousin to an associate to people who will clean your house and yards, to your average tattoo artist making money under the table to the hairstylist to the escorts, and much more to make money to survive and maintain a lifestyle of their choice. All who live in the streets disguise themselves as one person and act as another around others, yet you will never truly know a person until you stay with that person. You may know a person's ways and habits down to their walk and talk, but you will never know a person until you experience how it is to stay with that person and understand them.

To understand someone is to love them, something my Aunt Nessa said on her Instagram page. However, in the streets, the majority show fake love while the rest genuinely show no love. If you are a familiar face in certain areas, you are recognizable if someone tells a story pertaining to you. If not going by your reputation, you follow behind. Some show respect depending on who you are and what you're doing or did for that person. Again, they all go by your reputation. Most friends/partnerships are just personal business agendas for whatever business they are dealing with you, whether the fake friendships and what comes with it (sex, drugs) to those who want to befriend you just to get them high to spending your money. You realize no one wants to help you get the food, weed, liquor, cost of living, money, but people have no problem helping you lose it all, then watch them leave faster than they came.

Trust me, I've been there and done that, and I catch on to people and their b.s. since I'm far from slow. Everyone is literally out for themselves, and again, no one cares for the next. Some don't care about themselves simply because no one cares for them, for if they did, no one would be out here in these streets alone, let alone considered in the streets. Instead of showing love to other people like we although/should do in the streets, especially when you pay attention to those around you and what they say, how they think, what they do, and how they feel, they do the opposite of what we all want to feel in the inside. You begin to see everything you need to see to understand what you need to understand, besides the omens which are blind to the picture, or stupid/dumb/or simply insane to the b.s. They won't help you succeed in your dreams and goals and plans but will wish bad on you and consider themselves better than you. They have no technical goals, ambition, desires, agenda, rules, or traditions that they go by, for they have nothing to lose, so we become fearless, heartless, careless, trustless, loveless, and hopeless.

When you get/receive the lesson and learn from it by being in the streets, showing all that you regret doing in the past, it changes you into becoming wiser to some and evil to and toward others. Some get the lesson but don't change a soul. I, on the other hand, changed from all the countless mistakes/regrets I made in my past, from helping others while trying to help myself from my brother to my mother, to my ex-best friend, to all the roommates I had in the past to the niggas I used to fuck. I learned a lot being out on my own, for my own self in a city full of family and so-called loved ones on both sides of my parents' families. So the question should be, how should I now look at life after knowing what I've learned/been through (those who read my first two books understanding my mind and emotions, plus now being exposed to the life in the streets)? I've seen/experienced pain my whole life yet learned more from pain than I ever will learn from pleasure/happiness. I can't forget to mention accepting food stamps and a disability check becoming satisfied with a limit of food and money you are allowed to spend each month. I say fuck this lifetime and what all it has to offer.

I felt being happy, complete, satisfied was all a lie once I felt my first true pain, and it opened my eyes to what life is really about and how to live in the world in this lifetime, and it messes with a person mentally. Once you think differently, you begin to walk and talk differently. I once cherished and loved this life, but I now see it as a game. Since I'm an actress, I can act my ass off around others, especially under last-minute pressure. I act according to what others think since the majority is just as fake as a one-dollar pack of braiding hair and again want you there in their life for their own personal reasons. Little do they know I allow things to happen for a reason, and I don't tell everyone around me that I'm watching them. Yet, it goes in one ear and out the other of many, for I am clearly aware of why they jig with me whether it's for the money from doing my hairdo them thinking they are just smoking me weed with them not realizing I'm just using them to roll more blunts then what we're going to smoke.

Still, now I roll my own blunts with my one hand to people who will chill just to keep from boredom as if I got anything else better to do than watch them be fake in front of me and act like I know nothing, nor am I hipped to the b.s. that people try to throw my way.

People even tried to use my house as a sex house, thinking I let people stay with me, knowing all my experiences of staying with the people I stayed with in the past failed. I allowed people to fuck up my credit score by putting things in my name for the next person, from bills to a car, messing up my supposed-to-be perfect credit score. Then again, an average American credit score isn't as good as they first started with. People even thought they were using me for the free bus rides since I can get on the public transportation for free with another person, not realizing I ain't have nothing else to do. People stole money from me, and I was petty enough to steal it back. I always got something out of it, whether it was weed, or I had the money to buy the weed with. Shit, I even stole sixty dollars from a girl in my gym class, and only God knows why I really did it. At the same time, I got my karma back from stealing.

You always have to remain aware of a petty person, from stealing pills to catching one in the act of attempting to steal frozen chicken nuggets to one stealing my money order, and God got him back the same day, and I didn't pay rent that month. Then people always lie just to keep a conversation going between the two of you. Everyone always says, "they're here for you when you need them", yet no one has ever been there for me when I really needed someone. From food, shelter, and clothing (the three things you need to qualify as surviving in the world) and probably why I dislike money besides the destruction of earth cutting our oxygen supply low, nor will no one ever be there for you and me but God Himself.

The enemy came to kill, steal and destroy and that's what's been happening before your time. Again, understanding and realizing/feeling all this b.s., I'm disappointed at how life is as it is today. I feel sorry for some, tired of life and the b.s. I go through and couldn't care less for a person other than my three siblings on my mom's side and a few family members on my dad's side, and a couple of outsiders. However, I won't shed a tear for anyone besides when my papas die, my parents (I'm flipping when my mom dies), and a few cousins if I attend a funeral.

Anything or anyone I would have loved to help one another and change the world, yet more people are against me than with me, and since the world will play out the way God intended it to play out with or without my help, so why even bother? Therefore, the lack of love I give and have toward one another is great, and the love I expect to receive is unwanted. I have a permanent mean mug mark on my face from the feedback of those who see it, but it expresses how I feel as soon as I walk out the door. I'm on a mission to protect myself, watch my back, expect the unexpected, never believe what you see or hear, watch others around you and only be out of your house for missions only. It's like walking into the battlefield where only I have my back and give a care about me, love, will protect, provide for me, and do anything for me.

My mission consists of store runs for me and my house. If I'm not chilling with others smoking and drinking with my select few, I always do things with them. Now I limit myself to the parties I will attend since it is almost always some type of drama or unnecessary b.s. to pointless issues, and that stuff gets old fast. Again, when things don't add up, you subtract yourself. I will go to a family reunion, if not a birthday party, to some type of special event that I don't plan on staying for long (on my dad's side of the family). Afterward, I'm back at home, isolated from the world, where I get high and watch action or horror movies if not listening to music on YouTube or Pandora. Depending on who it is, I watch crime and comedy shows and will have a peaceful, successful day letting life pass me by. My phone is so dry I forget I even have one. I may have company over, and if we're not drinking and smoking turning up, then it's a guy companion there for my reason only. The plan is to have sex, but not all succeed, and some never will, so I play the part I need to play to get what I want, and like Martin telling Pam, "You ain't got go home, but you got to get the fuck out of here. Get to stepping!" Off to bed, I get ready for the next day I'll be ungrateful for life.

I check in on my siblings from time to time and stay to myself, for I learned a lot, and let's just say, the fewer people you hang with, the less drama you shall have. The more carefree you'll be, the happier you can get. To avoid future situations, I slowly separate myself only because I know I will not change who I became as a person and neither will the next, so forget them and what they have to offer for I'm out by myself, for myself. I stay away now on why we are in each other's lives, let alone around others, if we can't be/stay on the same page, especially if we're going two different paths in life. Why waste each other's time in continuing a soon-to-be-fail relationship? My time is valuable, precious, and limited. It's on a schedule, set goal, and time limit to do what I need/am supposed to do before meeting my creator/Most High. I'm very curious as to what he has in store for me. The relationship I've developed with Him, thanks to Him making me give Him my undivided attention to the many ways He did, is something I recently realized is amazing and the most peaceful thing any person can have.

Since I know now that this world isn't about me or others' wants/needs but about God and who He is, I no longer care to entertain others nor seek entertainment from others. Since this world wants me to live my life the way I desire using money, I've prayed to God that he'll lead me to get this money. That way, I can get what I need, do what I have to do to get it, live a little, experience things out of curiosity, do what I'm supposed to do in God's eyes, including changing my evil ways, habits, and prepare myself to die. I guess many people put and kept in the back of their minds that we all live this life to die, and honestly, I feel why and if only God would have taken me like the doctors assumed it would happen when I was an infant, yet he never invited me with him just yet. So since he didn't take me, I'll see what He has planned for me during the remaining time being here on earth since I now trust him completely with my whole heart. Even though sometimes I'm confused/lost at times, I still trust him. Want to know why? The famous saying *"what's understood doesn't need to be explained"* is the answer.

Being in the streets only changes you in two ways. Either become evil, hopeless, helpless, faithless, heartless, feeding to the devil and his wicked temptations, or become the others and search/seek for answers, looking for God and slowly seeking/ trusting in him. So I thank God from the top of my head to the bottom of my feet, from deep in my heart to the air that I breathe daily that I have a thing called life, and the lifestyle that I have now then what life I could have had for only he knows where I could have headed and because of my past I would have stayed there. Some people hold on to their past and the pain, not letting go of it, still living in the past, so they're stuck there. I just learned to use some of the past painful experiences for lessons I may need to know and understand in the future.

I want others who have pain out there to know that I, too, went through my share of personal problems/pain in the past, hoping to help change others from not making the same mistakes I've made. I want to help encourage the next person who needs encouragement to a shoulder to cry on, letting them know that we've all been there before at a time in our lives, and because of God, we're not where we could/should have been. I may be mentally distressed, disturbed to emotionally hurt to mentally tired after a short time I lived so far, but I learned a lot and came a long way and been through too much to be soft, afraid, hurt, limited. Not only do I have one hell of a story to tell, but all I've gone through fitted me for the things I shall go through in the future so that I may know what I need to know and understand what I need to understand and get the picture God has drawn for me to understand. I've learned what to do, how to do it, when to do it, and only rely on myself through God Himself. Like the tattoo on my upper back, I'm a walking testimony, and I can't say enough about God and how, because of him how much of my life then changed from the old me to the under-construction me and what all he has done for me.

Because of Him not giving up on me the many times He should have, I can't give up on Him and life, minus how I feel on the inside. Sometimes I want to give up and say screw this life and live how I want to regardless of what others say and think to the time I felt like killing myself, but through it all, God has been patient with me and has not given up nor let go of me. For as long as I have God on my side and through it all, I shall prepare and conquer what all life will throw at me since God is with me, and I trust Him even when I don't understand Him, I have to trust Him more. Again, I don't act how I feel. Instead, I'm a goofy, talkative, chill person who's always ready to party with loved ones, play cards, jig to music, all for the memories and laughter. I love to sightsee and do various activities from hiking to the movies to amusement parks to shopping to art museums to contracts, all with other people, and keep it pushing for the way it makes me feel on the inside. Anyone who ever met me, who thinks they know me, will all tell you I'm a chill person who just wants to have fun and loves my vibes. Unfortunately, I can no longer be as I wish, but as I need to be, and no matter who you are and what you do, we all must go through trials and tribulations for the pain, yet through my pain is where I started to finally understand God.

But God

Before I can say more, let me first tell you I may not know everything about God, for I'm not as wise I shall become, yet through the short time I lived, I've learned several things more through experience, for He shows you better than He can tell you. I first recently learned that love actually conquers all. Clearly, He shows us the act of love by using his only begotten son Jesus Christ, allowing him to get torture from spitting (which I fault a girl over) to getting hit with glass, to slaps/punches to the face to dying just so God can forgive us for our daily sins if we're sincere by heart. Through Jesus, we may be saved and have eternal life inheritance what God promised Abraham with Jesus Christ. Going back to the beginning, we were all born into this world, and as a kid, we never thought we were to die, nor pain, hurt, betrayal act as we get old. Everything you knew and saw and felt you expected to last forever, whatever it was and how it felt. No matter how life was as a kid, you never considered death. Do you think God just made us just to kill/allow us to die?

For those who don't know God or believe in God, explain to me how everything was first created, including humans, and don't say we came from animals, for it will still happen in today's life, and God is not Mother Nature. Explain where our "energy" will go once it leaves the body? As a kid, you immediately fall in love with the first person you were exposed to (usually the mother). It's every living things' nature to love something/someone other than his/herself no matter who you are or what you do. We all are made to love. Why are we born to love one another atomically? God is the definition of love, and He knows what it really means to love someone, and again, He shows us better than He can tell us. Neutrality we don't know how the world would be if it were the way it was supposed to be in the beginning, yet I know everything that comes from God is/shall/always be good.

If he knows creativity, aptitude, taste, flavor, talent, color, fruit (which I love so much), plants (weed), food period, plus how each of us is individually gifted people, then imagine how the world could be without the evil, wicked ways. For one, money wouldn't even be in the picture, nor jobs, down to the awareness of nakedness, so definitely life would have been smooth with no chaos, destruction of the earth, harmful to animals for I love chicken and fish, to the pollution. Think about the trash and when it's going to run out of places to leave the trash here on earth, let alone everything else left on earth, since we can't take anything with us. We can't continue the trash cycle because it will eventually backfire on us no matter what technology they may come up with in the future. After finishing its use, we will still be left with junk regardless of how many times you used the object/recycled it.

Throughout the book, I've been reading the bible and the two common commands God commanded of us (so far that I've read) were to first treat thy neighbor as thyself and to love one another. Those two rules alone should make the world spin, and we all can live peacefully and happily. This seems like a better place/reason to live since we would be doing the act of caring/loving one another, which is a good affection to have and feel among one another and not just relationship-wise. If we were to at least forgive people on the strength of what Jesus Christ went through and it's hard to forgive the next person, that's something I pray daily for to help me forgive others the way I need Him to forgive me for my countless sins. The three alone could have made life different for us all, regardless of your financial status or who you are. Yet we fail to care for one another, which starts many problems of all sorts, from jealousy to death to murder to betrayal, and once that begins, the cycle begins. Clearly, God doesn't like nor want chaos, so I believe that's why he made sins because if there was no such thing as sin, obligation, rules, regulations, whatever you may prefer to call it, then all sins will lead the world to self-destruct similar to how would have self-destructed if I had another lifestyle without my disability. Things may happen and change, but they won't last forever. With the chaos, nothing good will come of it.

We tend to think/assume everything to last forever, whether relationship-wise, friendship, money, food, or music. We act just like God intentionally meant for everything to last forever. Unfortunately, because of Satan, nothing in this lifetime will last forever, and that's the sad part. I believe I had to hurt and feel the pain to understand God Himself going through the pain and discomfort. Still, God gives us patience, grace, and mercy toward us all, yet we fail to use them for ourselves among others. Now what God does to us is it not real love or now? If that's not, please explain to me what is real love? On the strength of God going through pain himself, that's why we ought to go through the pain with Him as well. We all have to hurt and feel the pain to understand one another, especially spiritually, which we will fail to do, yet God won't.

Through all the stuff I went through in my past life personally, I know God was with me through it all, and only he saw me through, and without Him, I don't know where I would be today. God indeed works in mysterious, unique ways, and only He knows how to do things the right/best way and get your unlived attention when needed. I never paid attention to my actions as a kid growing up. Instead, I was more focused on how I felt inside and what all I was going through couldn't care less for anyone or anything else but my freedom, not thinking about how God felt about me, watching me grow up. My focus wasn't on God back then how it is now, and again, I went through pain to acknowledge Him. Although I didn't sign up for what's on my agenda, it strives me to say what God has planned for me and what he can do if I fully trust Him and change from my wicked ways. Just how God loved me through all my wrong, selfish ways, He still loved me and showed me His grace and mercy, and that's what we ought to do toward one another even though it will be hard.

However, since I've watched this movie called the *War Room,* it inspired me to give my all, including problems, to God and fully trust in Him and not take my life into my own hands, for my life now is in God's hands. Even when my faith isn't always there when it should be, God still works in His mysterious ways, and He'll show up and show out, and again He'll show you better than he can tell you. Again, I may not know everything about what God does or can do, but he has a way of showing/telling you things, and I love his sense of humor. God's very patient, tenderness, forgiving, merciful, kind, joyful peacemaker, a provider, a loving spirit, soul, energy that wants to feel important, loved, respect, worshiped, praised (how we praise and worship rappers, actors, our parents' act) and that's it. He simply wants us to live to love one another.

The three things that I consider us living are again food, shelter, clothes but the unawareness of nakedness I doubt clothes will really be in the picture how it is now far as wearing the latest trend, fashioned, name brand clothes competing to see who wears the clothes the best. There wouldn't be jobs as it is now, schools, set schedules that we all have to go by and witness what God has created for everything that comes from God in heaven shall be/remain good. And He knows what's all good and pleasing to us that'll satisfy us individually, for He makes things wonderfully nice. I even love the rainbow. Only He can make and create after the storm just because of what I went through in my past.

I know there must be a God and something to look forward to. I first need to understand how it is to have/be without and understand/realize my pain to appreciate what's to come in my future. The majority always, and I mean always will forever, take things/people for granted and will never miss it until it's no longer there/available, whether a spouse to a mother and daughter relationship to a best friend. I now know and understand how it is to feel unappreciated, alone, unimportant, unloved, and so isolated from the world that no one cares for you, praying for attention, awareness of my presence some things I believe God would/could have felt if He thought about not making the world for us and everything that's in it. He could have easily made slaves, food for him, entertainment for Him, including a wife of His choice, and call it a day, yet I believe He'll feel it wouldn't be enough to satisfy him. Those who are parents know the love of a kid and their parents, especially for the mothers who give birth to their kids.

Did you ever consider God's love for us as His children are close to how mothers feel about their unborn child? Both parents and God show their kids unconditional/genuine love. In my eyes, God just wants to father us all as a whole as his children by loving us and teaching us to love the next person as God loves us while He provides us with everything we need, which He'll go all out his way to make sure we're satisfied. Then there's the sex part that I love so much. It was a bonus to satisfy a person in a way I never thought about nor came up with. Neither would I have had the spirit of loving people the way God loves us, for He's a forgiving, loving, patient, caring, merciful, grace, and much more and in far from that/perfect and again I'm not right as an individual until I'm right with God.

I noticed/realized that God is not about his appearance but about the feeling you get inside when He's inside of you in your heart. The feelings we have and the tears that come with it, whether good or bad, are all the same, but the feeling of love actually over rules it all, and the definition of love is clearly God. We all know how He showed, shows, and will show. Seeing what you feel is a bonus is just as priceless as an object someone keeps in their home for their own personal reasons. I just truly, honestly thank God for all the good and the bad. Although I don't understand it all, that's where my trust and faith God gave me comes in and lets my future play out. However, it should play out.

I hope, wish, and have faith that all I've been through until 2014 will be better than what I shall go through in the future. Through it all, God has shown me what He can do/did do, especially when I couldn't see past certain days, including the time I was preparing for my death I was told to die on. Instead, God saved me through all my death experiences multiple times growing up and used me as one of his miracle kids and a walking testimony to others, including me. And just like the bible, the things I've seen, experienced, witnessed are just as real as the bible. God is/will forever be the realest thing life has ever offered, and God is the realest it can get, and I honestly forgot about that part. However, God still slowly did things to gain my undivided attention on who He is, what all He can do, whether I can imagine what He can/shall/will do in the future.

Not only did He get my undivided attention, but I watched in the front row as my life changed from one way to the next, watching closely on all that God could, can, and will do for us. There's a song I like to listen to saying, *"There is a soul that cries out in the silence searching for a heart that is desperate, lonely for a child that'll give Him his all, give it all for He wants it all."* All God wants us to do in return is to give us His heart fully, for He's not a partial God nor wants to receive anything partial. He wants us to fully trust in Him, have faith, and live right. We are to go through our trials and tribulations that'll lead you to your seasons of blessings to your purpose in life to fulfill what you were meant/designed to fulfill before God takes us home where we belong.

I also realized that this life is not a game or a joke, and neither is God. For Him to still have the patience to deal with us all, showing us grace and mercy on top of still blessing us is all amazing unconditional, genuinely, true love no man will ever show me in this lifetime. The icing on the cake was giving us Jesus Christ and us accepting and believing in Him as our Lord and personal Savior who died for our sins on a cross/tree in Calvary that through Him we may be forgiven for our daily sins. The sprinkle (my cassata) cake is the fact that we may have everlasting life with both God and Jesus (just as we assumed we were going to live forever being a kid growing up). Is that a gift/ blessing to have/give to the next? The simplest thing we can do is try to watch God do the rest as far as the walk, work, and talk even though we must long suffer since God Himself had to suffer for us, his own creation, just like a rebellious kid to their parent. We ought to accept all the good/bad and cry out to God and keep it stepping the best way possible.

God knows and understands it all, especially knowing us individually through our hearts. Again, what's understood doesn't need to be explained, and it's an understanding that there is a God, so there's no need to explain it, yet He does. So as long as God knows it all, I'm cool with caution due to the lack of awareness of what's to come next, which fear plays a role in. Remember, I've learned a lot, and I do mean a lot from pain than I will ever learn from pleasure, and we all have to feel the pain to understand it all, especially to understand God, why He's God, and what it means to be like Him. It's also there so we can appreciate all the joy that comes after the pain and the storm.

There's always a blessing in the storm, whether failed relationships to failed friendships, rejection, or acts. Not only is it a lesson out of the storms and situations, but it's what comes out of the storm with the lesson. It's not what you go through but what you get out of it. For most, the pain builds up from person to person who they need to become. It also lets another person understand other people's pain and saturation and for you to feel what others feel, and the most obvious thing is to feel what God felt to understand what He understands. We need to understand why He's God and not one of us. We need to understand why there is a thing called sin. Only God understands our minds and what they are for since we desire to know all God knows. Still, maybe that's for our own good to maintain human self-control (humanity), aptitude, controlling ourselves after being exposed to everything that God knows, for God made a mind for more than a few reasons, in my opinion.

There's a reason for even a God and a clearer picture of why He did what He already did/will do. Again, the love He shows us is incredible and more charitable than being unloved. Showing each other love, especially those who show genuine love is powerful, strange, and pleasant, including the act/feeling of being loved. Loneliness is a feeling you may bear, but no one wants to live life alone, let alone experience it. It's a feeling we need not feel. It's a feeling we naturally have within us to feel. It's the feeling of what you feel that is better than the sight you may see, so that you may cherish it. Trust me when I say feeling things are way better than feeling it, from sex to weed to being loved. The pain makes the person able to appreciate/accept and cherish what all love/pleasurable offers then not to experience pain at all, living life carefree/troubled less, worried less, for you wouldn't appreciate anything as you should appreciate it if you were to already know how it is to have but never imagined of having without.

When people grow into having everything they want/need, they won't fully appreciate it until it's gone. However, if they first felt how it is not to have/want something, once they finally receive it, they may have a chance to appreciate it regardless of what it is since they know how it is to be without. I have to be honest (and for those who read my two books) when it comes to things, people regardless of what/who it was, I could honestly care less about and never really cared about other people's hearts, just my own and the people I kicked it with to avoid my pain and issues. Take it from me. I now know how it is to have nothing, and when I say nothing, I mean down to the outfit on your back, and only when you're down to that last outfit do you realize to be grateful for what you have because you could have nothing. I was really ungrateful for clothes for the simple fact I always had clothes and assumed I would always have clothes, so why feel a special way about it? I have no reason I felt that way since it wasn't humble of me. Now that I know how it feels to have nothing from clothes to food to having no one to hear your cry, let alone help you in your time of need, I intend to appreciate the next thing I was to receive, regardless of what it was.

I know how it is to have nowhere to go nor have no one to call your own, including my family. If anything, you just wish to love someone only because we were created to do so, including feeling important to the next person. I know the actual definition of being alone. Honestly, it's peaceful, and truth be told, it's relaxing, and you get to focus on getting to know yourself, but you also realize you're missing something, not feeling complete as each day goes by. The being alone part isn't as bad as you having to live and die alone since no one wants to go through it alone, and it can mess with your mind, and you'd rather deal with it with someone else than be alone.

Newsflash: I dealt with everything by myself, from the brain tumor to my disability to trying to succeed in life. Again, all we want is to love and be loved. God put love (Himself) in us to have/use it, for, without love, people are pointless, worthless, and carefree. For me to appreciate things to loving people outside my family, appreciate a family of my own to appreciating the life I live now, I must first understand God and feel the pain so that I may hear His voice calling my name by showing/exposing/opening my eyes to the things and situation I was first blind to while He's with me. If I understand and feel the absence of it all, I'll understand and appreciate what's to come and what I once had that is no longer there. Again, I don't know what all God knows, but I don't think I should know, and I'd rather not know and understand it all but to just appreciate what's already been given to me and work for what I need and not for what I want/wish/ desire/ lust for whether it was a person or objects.

We all know and are aware that love is merciful joyful. A wonderful feeling in the insides is God and how He can make us feel. As His children, He wants us all out of love, which is a wonderful gift. Parents should know what I'm talking about as far as giving life to a kid you can call your own. The act of love given back and forth between two people is amazing, and that's all that God meant for us to do. We want others to recognize, respect, love, and appreciate the same thing God wants from us, yet we fail to show it to Him and others no matter who you are or what you do. The actual definition of love is not the same way we use it toward others. The point of a word is the definition of it. Am I right or wrong? Do we as a country use love the way God uses the word love? For some, we give partially, five, one-sided love while the majority is limited if not showing any. When God uses the word love, He backs up the word by defining it as the same love we ought to show toward one another, yet we fail to do so as a world, let alone a country. All we had to do was love thy neighbor as thyself as if you had the opportunity to love. Start yourself the way you desire to be loved and treated. If we do what we were told to do with common sense, it will bring joy, happiness, and appreciation to have a peaceful, joyful, productive day.

The next time someone says they love you, ask them if they love you the same way God loves you. If we walk together as a world, we can make it work. For with one, I am weak, but we can become strong with many. I can preach about this all day, but people will not agree and walk with me, especially since we have a need to love/lust things more than people in today's society still want to have an opportunity to want more/or what you don't have. Still, they will appreciate nothing until it's gone, whether it's the things we love or the people we need. We may love ourselves a little too much, developing pride (another of the seven daily sins), forgetting to humble ourselves on the strength we can also have without. That's where the pain comes in. After all Jesus went through, we ought to have many trials and tribulations, for we don't deserve what all God has in store for us all.

He loves us so much using the act of love, backing up the definition of love we're at where we're at in today's world, making our own decisions/mistakes while God still blesses us and the promises He keeps that He made to Isaac and Jacob. I firmly believe love itself can make the world go around, not money. If we did what we're doing now, shouldn't we all then be satisfied and happy minus the pointless wars we have to people belittling one another and much more that will result in chaos which is the story of violence? If we were to do it out of love, we would not only get the job done but also the feeling of satisfaction we tend the need to feel on the inside. No matter who you are, what you do, where you came from, or what you wish for, we all want the best of the best to the greatest of the greatest to its potential expectation, similar to how God feels/wants from us/wants to do jigs all, best of the best to great of the greatest. All we need is love to get the job done the right way.

Again, living in this lifetime, things aren't nor won't be as they should be, and we must long suffer to go through it all. Again, it's not about what you go through but what you get out of whatever you're going through. To love oneself is a contagious gift and can be a gift a person can continue to give. I can't put it in the right ways to express it, but it can be explained with actions. God Himself has blessed me with a heart to love/want to love/help others/become a problem solver when helping someone with a situation/problem. You know how it is to love a kid, especially your own kids and will do anything to protect them. You know how you give them rules/orders without explaining why there are rules since you yourself already know and understand why you did/said what you did/said to your kid? You know how you discipline your kids every time they disappoint you, don't listen to you, or what you say as you wished they did? Something goes when it comes to God and what all He commanded/ordered and yet still just like you'll protect your kids no matter what your kid did/done/will do toward you, your protection/love will never change for your kids, something when it comes to God from his love to his protection He shows/gives us daily.

I mean, what's the point of there being a god if we don't listen to Him or need Him? What's the point of being a parent if your kids won't respect/listen to you? That saying, "*you spare the rod, you spoil the child*" is so true. If you were never to get discipline, you'd continue to make the same mistakes/patterns, not caring about how you're making your parents feel and their wrath toward the kid's disobedience. Whatever it was to be that the child disobeyed you, without discipline, the child will become spoiled (rotten fruit that's not good to eat), ungrateful, unappreciative, and nothing good would come from it. Yet once the kid wears his/her own shoes to walk in their own path with their kids of their own having their own demands/rules ordering the same respect from their kids as your kids' grandparents wanted it from you realizing that the kids too won't listen and is repeating the disobedient cycle that you were repeating, feeling the same way your parents felt. The same way God felt at a point in time. Only then will they understand the principle of rules, orders, and sins.

We again don't understand what all God knows and understands nor what's meant for us to be, endure, live, do, accomplish. Just how we want the best of the bests to the greatest potential, expectations. It won't hurt to do your best. However, since we're mentally born to love, I believe and know God put us here to love Him first, then ourselves, then others and life would be free, the coolest place to be, living joyfully happy, and we all would have slept well at night waiting for the next day. Love is peaceful and is so powerful that it runs from one person to the next. It's a strong medicine/drug for anti-depression, loneliness, sadness, something I believe God didn't want us to feel or experience what He can feel, experience.

For example, suppose one person was to show their love to the next person. In that case, it can change that person's mood from sad to happy, and once the effect works on another, the domino effect is happening, and you can continue to show the love becoming the gift that you can continue to give. However you were to do it for whatever reason you did it, the act of showing love can change people from ungod-like feelings and trade them into god-like feelings. The only bad part about showing your love or acting on it is fighting the devil in his lustful, temptation, wicked ways. Our flesh lingers on, and because the flesh can be weak, it's vulnerable. My flesh is weak, but my spirit is willing to seek/keep God through me inside and out, not only that but the fact that God hasn't given up on me. Because of that, I've surrendered my life to God and gave my heart to his only begotten son Jesus Christ. They both are worthy of being praised. All that I went through and may go through in the future, what I'm going through now as up write this book can't be compared to what God went through/experienced. He shall bless all His people with one day using love, showing us his grace, showing us mercy by forgiving us for our wrong ways. That's His definition of love, not how we use the word love in our everyday lives.

This includes me being one of them who uses the word love to get what I want from the next person, not caring about hurting the next person. It can be from cheating on your spouse to the fake love I receive from both my parents, let alone my family. At the end of the day, the love we use is not the love God gives, shows us, already gave us by using his only begotten son Jesus Christ for again God is love, and his actions strongly back it up. The act of being loyal and faithful is what God does. His grace shows/will show us, but when we use those words toward one another is far from the same way God uses those words for, not only do we fail to be loyal/faithful to one another as a country, but we limit the faithful and loyalty toward one another to giving up on the next person, turning our backs on one another to having many mixed emotions toward one another daily.

However, when God says He is faithful, for He'll never leave you nor forsake you, He means that from the bottom of his heart, and He can't lie if He's our Lord. The definition of Lord is the act of exercising authority rights, having higher power over someone, and if God's Lord tells us to do things a certain way, how can He tell us what not to do if He's doing Himself? How can a parent tell/advise their kids to do something if the parent is doing what he/she told their kid not to do? Both the parent and God will become a bad influence, misleading us, so I now understand why there are rules, sins, boundaries, and limits. Not just to avoid chaos drama, but because God Himself doesn't do nor wishes to do so, why should He allow us to do things God wishes He didn't do, let alone us?

Again, because I never first tried to understand God (how He felt, feels before my time/ growing up as a kid to an adult and it's when after I was an adult that I learned, experienced, went through to understand it all and feel God through the pain and the pain itself. Not when I first felt pain but when I continue to feel pain, distress, and more unpleasant things. I knew as a kid how Jesus died, and I will forever strongly dislike/disagree on how He died, nor will I ever stand to watch it, and I really am emotional and sensitive about the whole situation and how it went down. I had to have something that both God and I can relate to in order for me to have that type of understanding of God Himself and the relationship He developed between the two of us.

I'll never understand why it happened the way it did, why it happened, or if just something different would have happened. Nor do I want to understand it since I'll forever disagree on Jesus getting hit, spit on, nailed, mocked, talked about, judged, laughed at, lied on, rejected, and much more and the point that Jesus had to feel/ go through all that and do nothing about it made me angry at everyone who played a part in it. For one, the things I name I would have easily fought a person over with, my one hand

and all. I dislike being lied to when no one believes you, talked about, and spit and hit on. God knows my granny put a spirit of a fighting warrior in me and others and how my mom was when she was younger the same way my little sister is right now as I write this book, it never takes much to fight, and there's no second-guessing it. That's only based on emotions that I'll feel based on another person.

So I was always quick to fight, but I am currently working with God on changing me and stopping the fighting. At first, it was hard and impossible to do, especially since I'm an upset, angry, very distressed person on the inside. Fighting will bring it out of me and add victory to the pain I feel on the inside. Then people fail to understand that a punch to the face is nothing compared to how my mom used to beat me every freaking day. Out of respect that she's my mom and the fear of God, I took and dealt with all the pain she caused me in the past and soaked it all in, so blame my mom on my mouth, aptitude, and my mind. I kept it pushing, hiding all the hurt/pain inside me, turning it to anger. The anger, however, was my secret weapon when it came to fighting, for that's the time I let my mind/body take control based on the anger it felt at the time.

The spirit just watches it as the flashbacks of all the pain/hurt I felt in my past when I was to go home daily, not a fist punch to the face or back. I wished my mom would have punched me instead of hitting me with the many different weapons she used to beat me with at the same time. I took that hurt/pain and used it to tolerate nothing from no one, yet I feel I was doing it the wrong way. Of course, I never really paid attention to me/my life. Still, after a while (recently), I questioned God by calling on his name, giving Him the chance to show up when I need Him, and so before I do what I usually would have done without thinking. Still, this time I called on God before I did what I wanted to do, and if He wasn't to show up, then God couldn't get mad nor blame me for my future actions nor judge me by my heart. Don't ask/tell me to make a change, for I will feel that I need to become the evil, crazy person my flesh desires me to be and is headed down that road.

What led me to question God with my doubt in the first place is because me going to prayer with the prophet I grew up to know told me I was mean, meaning God told me through his prophet that I was mean, and that was one of the many times I cried out to God. Still, it was too personal this time. For now, I felt unworthy of his blessings, grace, and mercy. I felt like He should leave and forsake me and never enter eternal life and inherit the blessing of Abraham. I felt He was disappointed with me, and I had failed Him too many times. I felt I was going to feel God's wrath. Yet, He allowed me to pray and cry out to God for forgiveness first and help fix what's all been broken inside of me and that everything ungodly-like that is in me to take from me an exchange for everything godly-like to be put inside me. I did this stepping process at the end of 2013, and although I listened to gospel music off and on, I really started to listen to it from September 2013 until this day as I write this book, and I'm glad I listen to gospel music more now than I did in the past. I do it to change the mood/ spirit/emotions I'm desperately trying to get rid of. It helps me think/focus on God for this world and lifetime is not about us but about God and what He's about to do in due time.

Things started to feel different, yet I still felt God was disappointed in me and everything I've done in the past. I felt ashamed to even present myself to God, let alone ask for forgiveness since I still felt unworthy. Then my trials and tribulations came while I was trying to change my life and focus more on God. The devil was messing with me, taking everything from me, making me regret my decision to change my life, and more pain came my way. My mind was really messed up, and I was about to lose my mind. I cried out to God two more times and told Him how I felt, what needed to be done and how I couldn't see past Thanksgiving of 2013 just the same way I couldn't see past May 2012 as I was in my storm. I had my faith and trust in God, but so was the doubt, and all I cared about was the hurt/pain I felt wasn't justified, and the hurt turned into anger. I never knew how God Himself felt the entire time, nor was I focused on Him. I still listen to my gospel music daily, but the pain, anger, sadness, and doubt were still there until fourteen days after the devil did what He did.

God showed up unexpectedly, showed out, and blessed me, for God knows what I want/need and how I want/need it. It wasn't easy through the storm, but neither did God say it would be easy. Plus, we as the world deserve nothing to be easy. I had my wrath, my evil thoughts, and anger. Through it all, God saw me through, and only He got me out of the hellhole I allowed the devil to dig for me. In fourteen days, I went from having nothing but an empty house with missing blinds to a house with a bigger bed than what the devil took from me with a table, a couch set with new clothes, and I became satisfied. Then, four weeks after the first two weeks, God blessed me with three couches another bedroom set, a recliner, and more clothes, and now I was satisfied. I was more satisfied because God knows I love shopping for new items, yet He also blessed me with more than the devil took from me. It's funny now that when

I was down to the outfit on my back yet again, I desperately called out to God. Only He saved and saw me through. Not a family member, friend, or loved one, but it was God all by Himself, for again, no one has been there for me nor will never be there for me as God is for all of us who believe/love Him. God proved to me that He is my provider of life, health, strength, food, shelter, and clothing, and again He can't lie. Again, there is always a blessing through the storm, no matter the situation.

I explained to you in many forms that there's always a blessing in the storm. The struggle is made for you to give all your problems to God, letting go of it all just to watch Him see you through on his time and not ours. No, it's not easy, for I'm a very petty, revengeful person. I have to let God take over and play the role He was meant to play in my life and let Him avenge for me instead of me doing it myself for vengeance is Mine says the Lord, and my God is faithful, honest, truthful, and loyal. I pray to God that He helps me and becomes the person He sees me as and not the person I and others think I am.

Less than a year, I was notified about the people who broke into my house, and I saw them suffer one by one. One girl had to give up her Section 8 housing to her son and niece, who broke into my house, causing the aunty to move back to the roach-infested house she tried to get away from. At first, the girl and cousin were out of town, but they came back to Cleveland. The third-party involved (in my house break-in) older brother got murdered before December 31st hit in 2014. That right there, I felt bad for the girl losing her older brother to gun violence. That was something I couldn't nor want to imagine with my older brother, for I might lose my mind. The girl Meka, who broke into my house, moved into her aunt's house, where she had to look for a job, which is hard to find in Cleveland. She went from having a car to losing it, going to food and blood banks to have food and money, having her son wear an ex-associate of mine daughter's diapers, destroying the house they were staying in. They got kicked out, having the aunty lose her Section 8 housing, and everyone staying there had to find other living arrangements. I was relieved that she was going through something yet not satisfied since she had help from her family to help her. Yet, in my case, I have no one but God, and fortunately for me, He's greater than all, so I was cool that Meka went through stuff. Still, I need for that dream I dreamed the day she did it to come true, and if I believe and wait on God and pray a little harder and longer than just as previous dreams come true, so shall this dream God allowed me to dream.

Again, the goal is to put and leave it in God's hands and that we all must go through pain to understand God's pain He went through/is currently going through watching us live in this god-forsaken world. He already solved his problem by allowing Himself to feel pain only to get a blessing out of it, which is Jesus Christ. And the forgiveness of sins for a chance of eternal life through Jesus Christ having Himself to feel the pain that I don't have the heart, soul to endure, nor the patience not to retaliate.

Again, there's a blessing in the storm, including the storm God had to witness and go through, and He's patiently waiting to put an end, and like after every storm of any kind, the sun always comes out, the birds, animals, and fish come to endure it all.

So again, if God went through it, we ought to go through it with Him. I'm far from perfect, and so is the next person, and I have a hard time not reacting to a situation whether I felt the need to ask God for help. God Himself went through the hurt, betrayal, jealousy, hatred by a close person He considered His closest (yet) before Jesus was created. I know now how it feels for someone close to you to be jealous, use you, envy you, betray you, to be untrustworthy from my mom to my ex-best friend to my brother. The three were the closest to me, whom I would have given them all my last if I had to just to make them happy, which will make me happy and appreciated on the inside. I once trusted them and loved them dearly, but things and emotions changed as the years went by. The difference from my mom is that I have to love her. I love her more than anyone on earth, including myself, and I'll forever love her. Yet, I'm not convinced that my mom genuinely loves me the way she can/ought to love me and I can't show/share my love with her due to the type of person she still is, yet I still love her, and God loves the both of us, and He understands what I fail to understand just yet.

My brother and I are trying to become close as we were before getting back on the same page on the strength that he's my older brother but more 'cause I love my mom three other kids that I grew to love. I'm glad the four of us are a part of my mom, let alone our granny, and that's the closest to completion I'll get to be. I understand why I have to keep them close. I pray that we all four reunite back in heaven with the same mom, grandparents, and the rest of my number one grandparents, four other kids, including my granny's other two sisters and their husband along with my great papa and his wife down to my cousins on my mom side of the family. I just want/need the family I once grew up with to know and love, and I need God to grant my wish and do what God wants me to do the best way I can do it. I realize that I'll never be satisfied until I get my family that was taken back. I miss the 1990s bad.

So back to the story. Since 2013, I've been seeking God more heavily, and through the year of 2014, God saved me and saw me through. Despite that, the devil was still provoking/tempting me. I ignored most of the temptations yet still fell for some, not realizing what I was doing and how God felt. Going back in the book where I talked about questioning my faith on two different occasions instead of fighting the people that I'll usually do without thinking twice when the opportunity presented itself, knowing I would release some anger and deep emotions. I usually don't care where I'm at to who I'm with. I was going to fight in remembrance of my granny and her orders.

The first time it happened, the devil was tempting me, and I was going to do what both Him and my flesh desired. However, the words that came out of my opponent's mouth changed me from the get ready to fight stage to calling out to God in front of everyone because I didn't expect my enemy to say what she said. Truth be told, it hurt not what she said but the person who told her what to say, so I then called out to God, inviting Him into the chaos to help prevent me from fighting, knowing I wanted to hurt my unhealed, emotional open wounds. Bad words can't describe what I pictured doing to her, and only God knows how I feel about what I'll do. This was the last stage before I did what I wanted to do flesh-wise, and only God knows how it would end if I did what I really wanted to do. Instead, I called out to God to listen for words and understood the convocation I wanted to have would be pointless, so I just shut my mouth (something I don't do) and said a few words my enemy wanted to hear. I literally sucked up everything and did nothing I wanted to do. Instead, I went from my regular playlist to my gospel playing Yolanda Adams' "Never Give Up," "I'm Going To Be Ready" and "I Got To Believe" in that order.

I played the music until I went home, where I prayed and cried out to God, even more confused than I thought I was. I was so mad/hurt that I went to prayer with a troubled mind, heart, and anger toward my mom instead of seeking comfort and healing from God. Instead, God let me know through His prophet that "He knows". Those were the only two words He spoke to me that night. I heard what He said but didn't let it marinate to understand that God knows and understands it all and feels my pain. Just like the songwriter/singer/producer Kirk Franklin says in his song "Wanna Be Happy?", *"If you're tired of feeling the same, if you're tired of things not changing, then it's time for you to get out the way, don't be stuck on how you feel, let Jesus take the wheel, He knows what road you need to take. It's so easy to complain, addicted to the pain, you give your heart they push it away, Jesus knows just how you feel, so let Him take the wheel, the love you (I) need He already gave, but it'll work if you want to be happy."*

I had to study and cry to those words of the song, and I understood what God was saying through the song, and it made me feel happy with a little joy, happiness. Still, the devil tempted me the second time, and this time I was going to do what the devil wanted to witness, knowing what my flesh and heart desired this day to finally come to pass. Yet because I questioned God where about with the lack of faith and with little doubt yet that didn't stop me from praying, asking, begging, hoping God would do something to fix this problem before I fix it my way, both God and I knew what I really wanted to do for He knows my mind and thoughts. I went deeper, asking/demanding God to intervene in me and the devil's plans and not for my sake but for the person I wanted to hurt very badly. At the same time, I was trying to do right by God and change my life and my old ways, finally giving all my problems and situations to God and working on leaving them in his hands. I also realized I need to do what I need to do to get what I really want — my family who died before me from my granny to my big cousin Murddy, since I have to go through Jesus to get my family back.

Even after praying to God all the way to the house where the devil was and preparing myself for battle after I just got done praying to God for a different outcome, I did not go into details (I shall do in the future in another book), but I prayed and talked to God the whole thirty minutes of being there. The devil did his best to tempt me, provoking me twice, and I was point two seconds away from giving in on the temptation, giving up on God and what I just prayed for, letting Him know I tried. I concluded that I would do whatever the devil wanted me to do and what I intended to happen, yet I still called on God one last time, thinking He wasn't going to see me through, for I knew how immature my open did not realize how big my God is. Let's just say God showed up, grabbed me, and took me home where I smoked my weed, watched a show, and had a good night's sleep.

Not a hair on my body was touched, and as bad as I wanted to fight, I was confused at first why it didn't happen to being surprised. God came and took me home, having everyone standstill around me, and I still had my little doubt and lack of faith. I was so confused that I just started thanking God for it all, for He understood what I didn't, and because He showed up on time tells me that He really cares for me, let alone his children. My lack of faith made the situation more precious, cherishable, and pure. Both times I questioned God. He showed me what He could do and that He has the final say no matter what the next person or I was to do/say. I learned that same week to forgive others. I realized only one person could have own my heart. The question is it Jesus or me?

Between God and myself, I've recently stepped down from the throne of my heart and am slowly but surely giving my heart to God's only begotten son Jesus Christ, so He shall have authority to sit on the throng of my heart. For one, I can't compete with God, and as they say, "if you can't beat them, then join them". I also want to give God a chance to understand Him and witness everything He can do for me, whether or not I can imagine it. There's only room for one person, though, to sit at the throne of your heart. I'd rather lose my life to God in order to claim it in the next lifetime through Him than to keep my life and lose it at the end living in the world and doing its evil works satisfying my lustful desires, doing what I felt like doing instead of doing what I need to do unless I want that express ticket to hell with a lighter fluid soul with my fiery anger and watch it all burn in endless pain of fire.

I'd rather not go down that road knowing I can do better with God on my side. Again, I'm not a perfect person, yet I'm on the road to bettering myself, giving up on my old ways/ habits. As you can see, I just turned down to fight, something I never thought I would do, but I called on God both times, including putting me in the most awkward position twice before so I wouldn't fight people from my dad's baby mama to my cousin. Now it wasn't me by myself but God that was with me at those times, and that's why I'm giving up theft fighting, for I had a list of people I wanted to fight, but as I write this book, I'm letting all that pass b.s. go and leaving it where I dropped it off. God also reminded me of my arm, surgeries, and the pain, so maybe I'll think twice before fighting the next person. My question will always be, is the next person worth messing up my health/definitely not. Now I have to be honest. God told me to stop fighting to how reckless my mouth was starting in 2010, and I never listened. For starters, He used his prophet to tell me about my mouth being a problem, and if I didn't listen and watch my mouth, God was going to take away my blessing, and after hearing Him, I still didn't change, yet, for my mouth was as reckless as a freezer keeping what's in it frozen. My mouth backfired on me, and since I knew I could fight, that was the main reason I ran my mouth in the first place, plus all the pain I felt on the inside.

Anyway, back to the story. The first fight in college wasn't enough to shut my mouth and stop the fighting nor change my aptitude and ways. Since I never changed, it led me to get suspended from college, and that was the blessing that got taken from me. I regret the actions that led me to the suspension. At the time, I didn't care, yet as I received my punishment for my violent behavior, God allowed me to get suspended and take back what was given to me, and I couldn't even complete the class I was determined to complete. Even after it was taken from me, I still didn't listen. Instead, I focused on my pain, hurt, anger and how I would respond to it all and deal with it. On top of that, I was upset, frustrated, and lost, so I started kicking it with different people still fighting in 2011. I went from fighting sisters to about to fight a former associate or three to a person. I almost thought I had to fight the one I considered my older sister Laisha to other classmates I fought with whom I went to high school. My mouth didn't change, nor did my aptitude, and I didn't care nor notice how God felt watching me, my ways, and my behavior.

Just like 2011, I brought 2012 in the same way, fighting former classmates to other associates, not closing my mouth. I still didn't care about anything but the pain, trials, and tribulations I was going through at the time, from me being homeless to me having only three outfits to the common betrayal of others from my mother to my brother. I wasn't paying attention to my actions at the time as to how I do now as I write this book. The one girl I fought in 2012 bit me on my left arm, and I'm left with a mark on my arm, but best believe I bit her back, digging my teeth in her skin tasting the blood and her skin, but I didn't stop until I felt satisfied. The last fight of 2012 resulted in a shoulder dislocation.

I never knew I even had an injury until I went to the emergency room for my vomiting problem, the doctors call Caves. Only at the hospital did I realize the discomfort in my shoulder, and after the pictures of my x-ray, I was told my shoulder was out of the socket. I was scared, shocked, and couldn't believe what was coming out of the doctor's mouth, let alone in my ear. The only best part about that was the going to sleep. However, my shoulder was still sore the next few days until it dislocated again as I slept on the floor at an associate house. After calling on God, I asked Him to fix it at the same time, massaging my shoulder in a curler position until the pain subsidized. Yet, I was afraid to move my shoulder, let alone do what I'd usually do before I started having problems out of nowhere. Through God's grace and mercy and help, He put my shoulder back in place as I was stuck laying on the floor, afraid to get up, let alone ask for help. Although God saw me through, the picture He painted for me was not yet clear to me nor revealed in my eyes, for I was still blind to what God was trying to tell me.

I chilled the rest of 2012 out, but in 2013, I was still in fights but not as many fights as I have been over the years. Although my shoulder didn't pop back out from my fights, it still popped out in different, unexpected ways, causing me to have two fractured bones, one at the top and the other at the bottom. That resulted in my surgery in August 2013, the same year I was going to change, but before I did that, I did my shares of mess and unlikeness in God's eyes and was careless in my eyes. After the surgery, God told me I was mean, telling me about myself, and I still did one more un-god-like thing. For my punishment, God allowed my shoulder to get dislocated again after my surgery two months later, and after going through that pain for hours, the doctors finally popped it back in place. The sad part was I had to get surgery again for the second time, so since 2014 was approaching, the first thing I was going to do was get my surgery over and done with.

Going through it again was emotionally and physically disturbing, yet I had to accept my fault and suffer for the sin I committed. I went through my next surgery alone with no help/support from a family to a friend or loved one, so I was left to suck it all up and roll with the punches. It's funny how the same people who left me to get my shoulder dislocated, being involved in their drama that had nothing to do with me, weren't the same people there when I needed them even after they said they were going to be there for me. I guess we all lie. When you need someone the most, they'll never be around but God and God only, especially in my case. Not one person can step up to my plate and say they did anything for me, but my mama, who was bussing it open and pushing me out, and my dad, who nutted in her. Other than that, no one can say they ever did anything for me.

By this time, I began to finally see the picture God painted for me, but I wasn't trying to look at it just yet. However, I still needed His help/grace and blessings, which He showed me through it all when I was right and wrong, and I love Him for that. The next time I was planning to fight, regardless of my two surgeries, stopped because of what the girl asked me. I first talked to my cousin, seeking guidance, then planned on seeing God's prophet. Yet, I was still going to head back to where God just delivered me from, feed into the devil's wicked ways, and would provoke the person to fight me, which would be easy for me to do since I could become a bully. I planned on fighting her, having her be admitted to the hospital, leaving a permanent mark on her since that's my signature move to do on people so they can remember why not to fuck with me.

However, God intervened on my plan by sending me back to the hospital that Thursday, knowing I planned to fight that Friday due to an unexpected pain preventing me from using my shoulder. No one understood the pain, but a picture that showed a piece that clearly is floating in my shoulder was spotted in an older picture, just a defined area. Of course, the doctors were confused, but I knew where the pain was coming from.

Long story short, God allowed me to get admitted for three days messing up my Friday's plan, still not looking at the picture God drew for me. All I wanted to do first was get out of the hospital to fight and feel better on the inside. I began praying to God to at least send me home, and I'd rest my shoulder. And after the therapist and RNs moved my shoulder for me, it caused the loose piece to move from where it was to back where it first was. Thankfully, the pain went away, and I could move my shoulder on my own with no pain. I thanked God but finally got the picture He painted for me back in 2010, well, since birth. He's been telling me to give up the fighting before I'd lose my only good arm left and be with no arms/hands since God can do that just to tame me. As many times as He told me, He knew I wouldn't listen, yet He found a way that will make me give God my unlived attention, and it's the shoulder of my good arm/strong arm that I fail to live without and would do anything to keep the one arm I do have now.

Again, I had to go through pain to understand the lesson and the moral of the story. I have to give it all up to save my soul and not perish. Like the bible says, *"If you have a hand that will cause you to sin, cut it off for it's more acceptable to enter eternal life with one hand then to enter hell with both of them."* I'd rather give up fighting to keep my life arm and maintain my own health than to continue to be hard-headed and lose both my arms spending the remainder of my life at a nursing home depressed, mad at the world, feeling useless, unimportant, unloved, unappreciated, regrets, herd, jealousy spirit envying others around me. Again since God knows this already, He allowed me to feel the pain so that I may understand/learn and listen to what's important and what's not important. Only then did I begin to change some more. When incident number two happened, I read my bible more and ran to God a little faster than before, giving Him the chance to save me before allowing myself to perish and destroy all who tried to destroy me, not caring how anyone was to feel about this. For it said (which is true) that you must be prepared to dig two graves on a road of revenge. One for you and one for the person you seek vengeance from. I would have been satisfied doing my revenge, but I would also be with the devil and his wrong ways and doings. Not only did God see me through, but I'm running to Him and latching on because I can't win without Him, and I must start by changing myself before I want/need others around me to change.

Again, I learned in the bible that I must first pluck the plank that is in my eyes that I may clearly see the plank that is in my neighbor's eyes and pluck it out successfully, for with my plank still being in my eye, I wouldn't be able to see correctly the plank that is in my newborn eye. I have to humble myself for the sake that God shall save my soul for his bigger and better purposes. My main question would have been, why did God save me, and what does He see in me, seeing I came from poverty just to experience the life I am currently in? I'm just glad and grateful that He now has my undivided attention. I will forever give Him my undivided attention if I want to maintain peace, joy, happiness, and prayer. With patience, I'm waiting on God for all of this to go past, and I can't wait. God will deal with the devil on his time, and since this is not my battle to fight technically but God, I'm gonna aggravate the devil by working with God against the devil and be good/proud of myself. I know it's not going to be easy, and by my body being weak, the spirit doesn't stop the spirit's wiliness and heart's desire.

That means since I'm willing to change and turn my life around, to do what is right the best way I can since I have to deal with the people in this world with me, that God will/can help me along the way since God is faithful and cannot lie. There was a demonstration done by my pastor R.A. Vernon from The Word Church that I watched as a kid, and as he said as well as the bible says, God is willing to save, pretext, help, change you, but you also have to really want it for yourself for God knows and will judge us based on our hearts. I believe I went through what I went through in the past to have a chance to appreciate, accept, and handle whatever shall come my way in the future. So,

I've been convinced enough to trust in God and everything, even though I may be currently lost as of 2015 and not where God will lead me. So yes, I thank my mom for all those beatings since a punch in the face has no comparison to the beatings, bruised, bent fingers, to the many dislocations of my shoulder. Because I dealt with my mom and her b.s., I can deal with it all if I choose to. Just like how I lost everything once, I dealt with it the second time, and if it were to happen for the third time, I'm now convinced that I can deal with it with the help of God nothing we were from nothing we can return for we're nothing without God.

It's other things that I went through that fit the person I am today and will prepare me for who I need to become in the future. It's my will to see what God sees in me so I can understand why He worked on me as much as He's already done from early as an infant to blessing me with more than what the enemy stole from me. What makes me so special that God had to create me, let alone leave His flock of sheep just to find me so He can bring me back to his herd, rejoicing that He found me? I consider myself the sheep that ran off (for those who read my books *Behind Every Smile and Walking Testimony*) that I first started decently being taught about God, but the pain I began to first feel distance myself from God when it was supposed to drive me near Him. Instead, God got my attention, found me, and is currently bringing me back to His herd of sheep as I write this book.

Only He knows who I will be in the next five to ten years from now and wherever I shall be and whatever I shall do in the future. It will forever be my job to trust fully in the Lord since God is not a partial God, nor does He do half things, nor is He lazy about anything. Since God took the time to do what He did for me, I have/owe/ought to finally try and give my all and keep it in his hands, for my life is in God's hands. Regardless of how I feel on the inside emotionally and how alone/abated I feel, I still have to trust and believe in God, and that'll He fix all my problems and broken pieces the way He knows it will fix me and not what I think I want/need. I'm just a girl who wants to love and be loved. Again, everyone was born to do and feel, yet I haven't shown God the love I ought to show Him in the past. Do I then deserve someone else's love when I didn't even show my father my unique love? Instead, I watch as God blesses me, which I took for granted and wasn't as appreciative as I should have been until I lost it all again.

If I never experienced how it is to have nothing, no one to cry to, or no clothes or food, would I have a chance to appreciate what was given to me? I really had a bad problem not appreciating anything, especially if I already had it. Every house that I ever moved from starting at eighteen, I will purposely leave items from clothes, shoes, beds, dishes, just simply because I had other things to make up for it and couldn't care less for all that I did have since I always played favoritism to what items I really liked to the ones I didn't care for. Then the party life I was once living in the past seemed like it smoothed the pain away, yet the pain was still there after it was over. I never gave my pain to God, and with all that I've long suffered so far, nothing changed until God made me realize that the focus was to be/remain on Him and always has been. Since both God and I are working on being on the same page, we're on our way back to the rest of the group.

Now, on the path back to the others, I must be fit to hang with the others again. I have to be willing to live for God and not myself so that I may have my life for the next lifetime when everything that God will create shall/always be good. That means I'm now working on myself (removing the plank from my eye), turning from my old wicked, petty ways, and loving God just as He loves me. My job is to give it all to God and watch Him show up and show out on His time and just like the Israelites coming from Egypt as slaves to owning their land far out and watch Him bring me from point A to point Z.

Again, it's not about where we came from but where we ought to be. There's always a blessing in the storm, even when you don't see it just yet. Jesus is the blessing in God's storm He had that we all deal with together. So since God had to deal with the devil, He decided to put a blessing in the storm so that we may know, accept and appreciate all that God has/will do for us all. The simple rule was to love one another and treat thy neighbor as yourself, and no matter how strong, boldly I speak about this, the world as a whole won't change since what's in God's will has to happen for heaven and earth shall past, but God word will stay forever for his words should not return void. So, this life has to play out the way God set up the pieces to his chess game, and He needs no one's help to finish this game, for God's last move will be the best move. Meanwhile, as His children, we ought to get right with God's desire to please Him just like how we tend to please our parents. Make them proud in a way you know how to make your parents proud, whether it's following in their footsteps to finding yourself, and having your parents support you every step of the way.

We all ought to want and try to please, trust, believe in God and give Him a chance to show up and show out instead of waking us up in the morning to control our organs on the inside since we have no control over our organs/immune system. Regardless of what I've felt, gone through, learned, and experienced, I can try. I'm willing to do my best and so should the next one. I focused on prayer, then the bible while praying for more wisdom and understanding of what I'm reading in the bible, for some can take things out of content due to lack of wisdom. Then I pray, something I've always done, stopped two different times, and recently started back up in 2015. I can no longer allow others to sidetrack me, and neither should you, regardless of the situation or circumstances.

Everyone has a story to tell, paths only they can walk that fit them, and what we do with the past is up to us to determine our future. I can easily go back to partying, living off the government, and scream f*** like but on the strength of God believing/seeing something in me that I yet not see, I ought to know what He knows, see what He sees, and understand what God already understands. I ought to give Him my all, and He'll fix the rest, so by the time I regroup with his flock of sheep, I'll be ok not to run off again. Again, it won't be easy, and it was never meant to be easy. It's to build us and prepare us for the future, for no matter what we were to plan in the future, what God allows and won't allow still plays out for our sake and for the ones who don't care or won't try to believe in God or his Son. Like Jesus said to Judah, "It would have been better (for you) if you never existed."

I will feel bad for some but not sorry for none. If I can work as hard as I am working, so can the next, and there's no excuse. Again, for the last time, we all must go through our trials and tribulations to see God work in the strange/unexpected ways He does, and when He does it, He's never late. Again, our time and his time are different. Since numbers don't end, I will never try to keep up with my age nor the next lifetime, nor will I care for a birthday, only this lifetime should I care about it. Anyway, no one can go through what we go through individually the same way we did. If that weren't the case, the next person would have had your path. Our unique paths were already chosen for us. We, however, decide on how to walk down that path. It's hard to stay encouraged, especially when you have no one to encourage you, yet you pray to God to fix that problem and encourage yourself. You have to speak life within yourself, speak your future, and believe that it's already done for your tongue is like a curse, so you need to claim your victory in the name of Jesus, believe, sit back, and live for God and watch He'll see you through.

The blessings will come, but so will the pain. The pain brought me from the party, sex, drugs lifestyle to back on God, and the devil will try to tempt you. Yet God has the final say. Again, if I recently decided to trust in Him fully, so can you. You just have to believe and rebuke the devil in the name of Jesus Christ to stand behind you, and not infrequent of you, for you are the heads and not the tail. However, through it all, we can bear it with God on our sides, but we have to long suffer considering what all Jesus went through for us all. We have God with us, through us, and with Him, we shall make it and conquer the devil, his wicked ways, and his evildoers in Jesus' name. For God loves me so that I'll never know the precious lamb of God.

Amen.

Made in the USA
Middletown, DE
06 March 2023

26177300R00156